T0340011

BETTER CUSTOMER SERVICE

This readable and concise research-based book discusses seven simple rules that will help businesses and individuals improve their customer satisfaction and workplace environments – and make the world a little better and more pleasant.

An author team with extensive cross-sector experience provides a foundation that will help improve customer service no matter the type of organization or situation, allowing customization according to industry standards and expectations. Although the basic steps are simple – going all the way back to preschool and kindergarten – they can have a significant positive impact on customer service and on basic human interaction. If an employee follows these simple steps, not only will relationships with customers improve, but so will relationships with co-workers, increasing overall organizational satisfaction. Readers who adopt the principles in this book may find that their personal relationships improve as well.

The primary audience of this work includes any business that desires to improve customer service. However, anyone who works with people will appreciate the conversational tone and specific illustrative examples in this clear and immediately actionable book.

Edward C. Brewer is Professor of Communication Studies and directs the Communication Studies Online program at Appalachian State University. His research includes over 20 peer-reviewed articles and book chapters. He has also authored or co-authored three books.

Terence L. Holmes is Professor of Marketing at Murray State University and chairs the Graduate Business Curriculum Committee. He has published peer-reviewed articles and cases in journals and textbooks. Prior to his academic career, he was a corporate trainer and co-owned a private vocational school.

BETTER CUSTOMER SERVICE

SERVICE

Simple Rules You Can Apply Today

Edward C. Brewer and
Terence L. Holmes

Routledge
Taylor & Francis Group

NEW YORK AND LONDON

First published 2021
by Routledge
605 Third Avenue, New York, NY 10158

and by Routledge
2 Park Square, Milton Park, Abingdon, Oxon, OX14 4RN

Routledge is an imprint of the Taylor & Francis Group, an informa business

© 2021 Edward C. Brewer and Terence L. Holmes

The right of Edward C. Brewer and Terence L. Holmes to be identified as authors of this work has been asserted by them in accordance with sections 77 and 78 of the Copyright, Designs and Patents Act 1988.

Library of Congress Cataloging-in-Publication Data
A catalog record for this title has been requested

ISBN: 978-0-367-75737-3 (hbk)
ISBN: 978-0-367-75733-5 (pbk)
ISBN: 978-1-003-16376-3 (ebk)

Typeset in Sabon
by codeMantra

THIS BOOK IS DEDICATED TO THE
ESSENTIAL WORKERS AND MEDICAL
STAFF THAT PROVIDED CUSTOMER
SERVICE DURING THE UNCERTAIN
TIMES OF THE COVID-19 PANDEMIC.

CONTENTS

PREFACE

We wrote these guidelines before COVID-19, but as we have reviewed our seven rules, it is clear that they apply to emergency situations and to businesses reopening from the sheltering-in-place orders or other recovering from disasters (hurricanes, etc.). Here we address the seven rules with some specifics related to responses to the pandemic. On our website, customerservicerules.com, we also offer some resources especially helpful for businesses seeking to reopen after temporary closure for the pandemic or other emergency.

Come to class prepared

It is not just important to clean and sanitize, but it is important to display the approach you are using to do so in order that customers, clients, vendors, etc. (and employees!) know what you are doing and can be comfortable that you are taking their safety seriously. You want everyone to feel safe as you continue to provide the great customer service you have become known for. You may need to provide or require masks, limit the number of people in an area, or provide markings that encourage appropriate social distancing.

Complete assignments on time

Be sure to inform customers about extra time that may be involved in providing safe customer service. For example, extra cleaning and sanitization policies may preclude other tasks from being done, at least in the same timeframe as they were before the non-emergency environment. Make sure employees and customers alike understand the procedure and time expectations for new conditions, such as curbside pickup.

Pay attention

Be watchful for changes in CDC guidelines or other agencies that monitor the health and well-being of employees and customers during and after an emergency. Pay attention to what is happening to your employees and the community. How are interactions impacted? While attention to nonverbal communication is important at all times for the best customer service, it is imperative at this time. Be watchful of how your employees and customers are responding to changes. Brainstorm with employees to generate ideas of what special needs are important for your firm.

Show respect

Be sure to acknowledge individual wishes, especially if such preferences on the part of employees or customers preclude them from working under emergency conditions or from being able to receive services under your existing conditions. Show respect for the concern employees and customers have for safety, even if you don't agree on the extent of precautions. Err on the side of being more cautious.

Be courteous and kind

Demonstrating understanding and respect is even more vital in times of uncertainty and, in the case of situations such as the COVID-19 pandemic, sometimes fear. Instead of not knowing if people within your organization and customers are under stress, assume that they are in these challenging times. Overt, though not overbearing, expressions of kindness can offer a calming effect. If your employees must wear masks, brainstorm with them to try to discover ways they can still use nonverbal signals. If they do not already have a photo ID displayed, perhaps you could start doing so and/or include larger pictures of them so that customers can better relate. The role-playing application is especially important under these conditions, allowing you to try out customer service practices under the new guidelines and with new elements, such as masks.

Follow directions

Being prepared is very important, but if there is no follow-through regarding that preparation, then service failure will likely follow. Besides posting guidelines for your particular type of operation, you should have regular meetings/reviews with employees to ensure everyone understands current guidelines and how to proceed under them. It is even more important that the directions your customers need be clearly displayed and everyone in your organization must be fluent in explaining them. The flexibility your employees need to enable great customer service can still exist, except where safety protocols need to take precedence.

Always do your best

Collecting data on service activities is even more important. Monitoring service time, quality standards and results, and customer satisfaction is imperative. Comparing data to your competitors and striving to be the best continues to be the goal. The template in Chapter 7 should be used in meeting with employees and perhaps with a sample of customers, specifically to investigate thoughts about the current environment, changes, and fears.

The techniques we offer in this book are backed up by research, and following these guidelines will help you improve your customer service in any situation. These simple rules apply across the board, but paying special attention to them in regard to the emergency situations could set your business apart from others and help you to stand out as a beacon of great customer service in times of distress. We trust you will find this book helpful and easy to follow. You can apply these rules today as you lead your organization in improving customer service.

ACKNOWLEDGMENTS

Ed would like to thank Robert Fulghum for his book titled *All I Really Need to Know I Learned in Kindergarten*. Though they were enjoyable, it wasn't the essays so much as the title of the book that got Ed thinking about how simple the rules of good customer service really are and that we actually learned them in our early years of school. And he would like to thank Terry for his friendship and collaboration over the past two decades. Ed would also like to thank the Boulder Dam Credit Union in Boulder City, Nevada, for its example of "outrageously superior service." He has thought of them often as he considered how to apply these simple rules. And, of course, Ed would like to acknowledge his wife, Pam, and their daughters, Elizabeth and Emily, for love and support throughout the years.

Terry would like to thank Murray State University for the sabbatical that allowed him to begin working on this project with Ed. He would also like to thank Ed for the years of joint research that have led to many satisfying outcomes, both professionally and personally. Terry would also like to acknowledge the love and support of his wife, Robin, and their children, Ian and Victoria. Finally, he would like to acknowledge the late Bob Dwyer (BD), his PhD program mentor. BD simplified marketing as being about how we ensure we get people what they need, and building relationships while doing so. This perspective was a solid foundation as we developed the simple rules in this book.

Thanks to Meredith Norwich, Senior Editor, Julia Pollacco, Editorial Assistant, and Julia Hanney, Production Editor, for their comments and help with the production of this book.

INTRODUCTION

All of us have first-hand experience with receiving customer service and, whether directly or indirectly, most of us have experience in providing such service as well. You're reading this because you're likely seeking to improve your professional and/or personal capability to communicate better with others and serve them better in different ways. The two of us have had both personal and professional experiences with customer service both prior to and during our careers in academe. We have worked in the service industry, churches, retail, banking, and training and development, to name a few. Our research on improving communication within and between organizations has built on that experience and given us valuable insight into many aspects of customer service. We talked about ways of sharing that insight so that people in any type of customer service position would be able to apply it and improve customer service in their organization. This book is the result. Throughout the chapters we present ideas, models, and concepts that have been developed through longtime research and practice. We have laid everything out so that you can easily and quickly apply them in your own customer service setting. Included are many anecdotes from our own and others' experience with customer service, both good and bad, to make the concepts and models relatable.

"Customer Service," Then and Now

What is customer service? What experiences have you had with customer service? What prompted you to purchase this book? Does customer service mean the same thing today as it did 40 years ago, or even a decade ago? You are about to read about some simple rules that will help you and your organization offer the kind of customer service that can set you apart and, we believe, strengthen your customer relations and increase your business.

Consider Ed's experience with customer service on a trip from Ohio to Florida when he was a child, and then a number of years later when he was a parent:

We were traveling to Florida from Ohio in our 1964 Dodge Station Wagon (with no air conditioning). We stopped at the Texaco service station (yes it was called a service station). Dad rolled down the window as the attendant, dressed in the Texaco uniform (and smiling, looking like he enjoyed his job), approached and cheerfully asked, "How may I help you this afternoon, sir?" Dad said, "Fill 'er up please," and the uniformed attendant began filling the car with gas. The attendant then asked if he could check the oil. Dad said that wasn't necessary because he had just done so at the last stop. The attendant then noticed a dirty windshield and washed it. Then he checked the air in the tires. At the time, Texaco touted 22 services they offered to customers who came in for gas! My brothers and I got out and ran inside for a bathroom break. Mom pulled out a half of a sandwich (we could choose from peanut butter and jelly or ham and cheese) and a small juice for each of us. Ten minutes later we were on the road again.

Fast forward 35 years, and I thought about that childhood experience as I was traveling down the interstate from Ohio to Florida with my own children, in our 1999 GMC Safari van. I stopped for gas at a "convenience" store (notice it is no longer a "service station"). I got out of my van and stepped in a puddle of coffee someone had spilled and several pieces of trash stuck to my shoe. As I tried to shake them off my shoe, they blew under the van. Next, I discovered the credit card reader at the gas pump was broken, so I got back in my van and moved to another pump.

This credit card reader wouldn't read the magnetic strip on the first card I tried. Fortunately, it read the second card, and I typed in my zip code. After filling up (and checking my own oil and washing my own windshield), I waited for my receipt. The card reader flashed, "See cashier for receipt." So, I headed into the store and waited in line to request a receipt for the gas that I had just pumped myself. The cashier simply handed me the receipt without a word, no indication of being sorry for the inconvenience or that someone would go take care of problem at the pump now. I didn't even get a "thank you for your business."

Why has good service given way to poor service, or no service at all (the euphemistic "self-service")? Cost is one concern. The infrastructure needed to enable provision of excellent service is expensive to maintain, and quite daunting to consider if your firm doesn't already have at least some pieces in place. However, many excellent customer service experiences stem neither from slick physical settings nor from high-cost data systems. Rather, they are experiences based on how people from a particular firm treat a specific customer that *exceeds* what that customer expected. For example, a *Consumer Reports* (Gikas, 2017) article on cellphone service providers explains that the most satisfaction with customer service is with smaller carriers, not the largest national competitors. Reaching such outcomes more consistently in your own industry can be done through some pretty basic plans and actions based on the rules we present in this book – simple rules that you most likely learned in preschool or kindergarten.

A few years ago, Ed read Robert Fulghum's book *All I Really Need to Know I Learned in Kindergarten* (Fulghum, 2003). The book is full of interesting essays, but it is the title that kept coming back to his mind for the next several years. Each time Ed experienced customer service that was less than satisfying, it occurred to him that simply following some of the simple rules we learned in kindergarten or preschool would have allowed the service provider to resolve the issue pleasantly. Even if an agreement was not reached, following such rules would lead to a more positive, if not completely satisfying, experience.

Thus, we want to offer in this book a set of guidelines for customer service that are straightforward, commonsensical, and simple. In other words, we offer guidelines that are easy to translate into actions for improving customer service in your organization. Along the way, we will introduce some simple but powerful tools that you can apply in your own organization. These tools will help you build a great customer service system.

We began by thinking about the simple rules we learned in our early school days and how they might be applied to achieve great customer service. We also looked at preschool, kindergarten, and elementary school websites to see what qualities are being emphasized now. What did we find? It was gratifying to see that since the days we were in kindergarten not much has changed! The goal in preparing young people for life is, happily, to instill an inclination to do the right things in interacting with others and doing individual things well. Though dozens of down-to-the-last-detail rules appeared across the schools we reviewed, there were several noticeable overriding themes. We decided to focus on these "consensus" rules as the basis for improving customer service. Here are the seven simple rules we will present and explain:

- Come to class prepared
- Complete assignments neatly and on time

- Pay attention
- Show respect
- Be courteous and kind
- Follow directions
- Always do your best

Let's revisit Ed's service station example for each of these rules:

- Come to class prepared – The attendant was ready to service the vehicle. He asked about any special needs, had his rag at hand and squeegee at the ready, demonstrating an attitude that he was ready to help his customer.
- Complete assignments neatly and on time – The attendant was dressed in a uniform and immediately came to the car. Motorists who arrived at such stations didn't have to go in search of a person to help; they didn't even have to leave the vehicle unless they wanted to do so.
- Pay attention – *The attendant noticed the dirty windshield and cleaned it without being asked.*
- Show respect – The attendant addressed Ed's dad as "sir." He respected his wishes not to check the oil.
- Be courteous and kind – The attendant was cheerful and respectful. Once everything was done and the motorist was about to pull away, the attendant thanked him for his patronage with a smile on his face.
- Follow directions – The attendant filled the car with gas but did not check the oil because he was told it was not necessary. The attendant was ready to help. He listened for cues and sought to satisfy the customer (Ed's dad).
- Always do your best – The attendant was neat and watching for ways to meet the needs of the customer.

Now let's revisit Ed's trip 35 years later.

- Come to class prepared – *There was no one there to help, and the machine was broken.*
- Complete assignments neatly and on time – *Apparently the receipt paper had not been refilled, and they didn't seem anxious to fix it when it was brought to their attention.*
- Pay attention – *There was no indication anyone had noticed the broken machine or printing paper that had run out (or the trash around the pumps).*
- Show respect – *The cashier showed no respect for Ed (or even acknowledging him except to hand him the receipt).*
- Be courteous and kind – *The cashier in this case was not necessarily rude, but he was certainly not all that courteous or kind. A simple "thank you" would have been easy to offer.*

- Follow directions – Since it was "self-service" Ed was doing the work, and didn't do anything wrong. But surely there must be directions for store employees to keep receipt tape in the machines and the lot free from trash.
- Always do your best – Were employees doing their best if the machine was broken, paper was missing, and trash was all around? Is it doing your best if you don't even demonstrate to the customer that you appreciate their business?

The contrast in these two experiences is striking! We believe an organization that follows the simple seven rules we offer can develop customer service that will not only satisfy customers but also usually make them happy and likely to return to your organization again and again. In the "self-service" model, the customer provides the service. So, what could you do in your business to offer service in such situations? We have demonstrated in the scenario above how following the simple rules, even in small ways, can lead to a much more satisfying customer experience.

Let's look at two additional examples from Terry's experience:

I-9 form

I taught classes at several area universities for extra income during the latter part of my doctoral program. In preparation for teaching a night class one fall semester, I needed to visit the human resources office the night of the first class meeting to complete paperwork, including the immigration form commonly known as the I-9. I couldn't find my birth certificate to go along with my driver's license, so I took my U.S. passport instead.

I approached the window and told her my passport had expired the previous month (I had gotten it ten years earlier preceding my wedding in case my wife and I decided to take an international trip for our honeymoon. Busy with school the past couple of years, I hadn't taken the time to renew it.)

"I can't take an expired passport," the woman said through the service window.

"I couldn't find my birth certificate so I thought this would be OK," I replied.

"Just come back next time with the birth certificate."

I left the window and went to the lunchroom area to have a bite to eat before my 6:00 p.m. class start. As I ate a sandwich, I looked over the I-9 form and noticed something both the university worker and I had missed. I couldn't believe we had overlooked it, as now it fairly jumped off the page – "Acceptable forms of identification include U.S. Passport, expired or unexpired." (Suddenly it made sense to me, as you have to prove your citizenship to get a passport in the first place, so it being expired doesn't mean you are not a citizen anymore.)

I looked at my watch (ah, those pre cell phone days!). There was just enough time to go by the human resources window again before it closed and still get to the classroom before my students started arriving, so I hurried back to that office.

"Hi again," I said, to the same worker I'd talked with before. "I noticed on the form it says the passport can be expired or unexpired." I passed the form and the passport through the window and smiled. She looked it over for a few seconds, but did not look very happy, which surprised me, as our somewhat joint problem was now solved. I was surprised, that is, until she replied: "Well, I guess I'll have to take it then."

Looking back at the episode now, in the context of the seven rules, I can tell I probably fell short on a number of them myself. Among other aspects of my preparation, I should have paid close enough attention in the first place and initially approached the window with the "expired passport" part of the completed form circled. However, regarding the customer service provided that evening, I think the university worker fell even further short, perhaps on all seven rules!

Contrast that example of how bureaucracies provide "service" with Terry's more recent experience:

Chick-fil-A

My wife and daughter and I were traveling from Murray, KY to Atlanta, GA on a Thursday afternoon for an audition our daughter had the next morning. We stopped for dinner at a Chick-fil-A in Murfreesboro, Tennessee. Because we had a coupon for a free sandwich we decided to order only two full meals and split the waffle fries among us. To have a few more fries to share we upsized one of the meals to include large fries. The order came to the table while my wife and daughter were still in the restroom, so I started taking the food, napkins, and sauces off the tray and placing them on the table. I noticed that the upsized fry box was under-filled and held it next to the regular fry box in front of me to compare. They had about the same number of fries. I must have had a puzzled look on my face because I noticed a young manager glance at me as he walked by, and then he turned toward me without breaking stride and approached the table.

"May I help you? I noticed there must be something wrong."

"Hi. Yes. We got the larger fry with one order and it isn't filled all the way."

"Let me get that for you," he replied.

I thought he might take the under-filled box with him to add the proper amount to it, but he was away in a second without doing so. In about a minute he was back with a small order of fries on a tray.

"I apologize for that sir," he said as I thanked him for fixing the problem.

Without asking, only seeing a customer showing a sign of something being out of the ordinary, this person took the initiative, asked what was wrong, and corrected it, all in less than two minutes.

In preparing you for the remaining chapters, we feel it is important to review a basic common fact underlying the noteworthy service excellence achieved by some organizations. Think of world-class service and what names come to mind? Disney? Nordstrom? Some local or regional firm you've used for personal or professional services? Regardless of your own answer, it is a safe bet that a given firm that has achieved a reputation for exceeding expectations for service and has, in fact, *inspired* customers and caused them to voluntarily mention their experiences to their family, friends, and colleagues *is focused on customer needs as its top priority*. This focus on customer needs as the driving force for the organization is known as the *marketing concept*. Other descriptions of it include market orientation, customer-centered, and other similar terms. But what, exactly, does it mean? Do you have to attend specialized training? Do you have to earn a degree in marketing? Are high-paid consultants necessary to develop great customer service in your business? Fortunately, you don't have to do any of those things! Rather, you'll be happy to know that, since you are reading this book right now with an idea that it may help you improve your organization's customer service outcomes, *you already have the right approach and mindset necessary to instill such an approach of great customer service in your business*. How, you ask, can that be?

The *marketing concept*, simply stated, is the philosophy that understanding your customers' needs and wants, and then providing the products and services that will fulfill those needs and wants better than your competitors can, is the very basis of your existence. Sometimes the concept is broken down into the four areas where marketers can apply strategy and tactics to compete; these are the "four Ps" of marketing – **products** (including services), **place** (channels of distribution, or the path products and services must take in order to be available), **promotion** (advertising, public relations, publicity, personal selling), and **price**.

However simply the marketing concept philosophy can be stated, the *reality* is that it is extremely difficult for most firms to instill it in every part of the organization. "Every part" means *each and every employee* in *each and every position* across the *entire realm* of operations. As

A Simple Diagram of the Marketing Concept

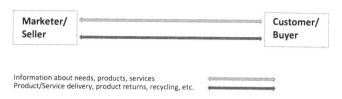

Figure I.1

many have stated, marketing is not just the business of a marketing department. Among the many functions of an organization very few tie so closely to the marketing concept as does customer service. To get the most from the guidelines, concepts, and models we present in the remaining chapters, you must first instill this customer-first approach in everyone, whether their customers are fellow employees (aka "internal customers") or your current and prospective customers.

Let's look at an example from the sports world that reinforces the idea that the right attitude must penetrate the entire organization. Frank Martin, head coach for the University of South Carolina men's basketball program, was asked about his team's top-rated defense during their tournament run to the school's first-ever Final Four appearance in 2017. The question was about which was more important – defensive *technique* (such as particular plays or player skills), or *attitude* (i.e., the mindset of "defense first"). Coach Martin answered immediately and unequivocally that attitude was more important. With player buy-in that defense comes first, the various skills and plays could be taught, practiced, and perfected because the unifying goal was an ever-present guide.

Techniques and tools for enabling great customer service to be delivered likewise depend upon your employees buying in to the fact that customers are the reason their organization, *your* organization, exists. We hope your own customer service attitude is already well on its way to permeating your entire organization. The rules in the following chapters are presented as helpful guideposts for customer service improvement journey. We wish you all the best on your journey to exceptional customer service!

References

Fulghum, R. (2003). *All I really need to know I learned in kindergarten*, 15th anniversary edition. New York: Ballentine Books.

Gikas, M. (2017). Have more fun with your phone. *Consumer Reports*, 82(3), 48.

1

COME TO CLASS PREPARED

"By failing to prepare, you are preparing to fail." – Benjamin Franklin

Our daughters were in the Girl Scouts. The motto of that organization is "Be prepared." We also learned the importance of being prepared in kindergarten. This still seems like a good idea, although certainly not everyone providing customer service seems to feel that way! We remember the emphasis on preparation and common sense. This was true in our schooling as well. Coming to class prepared made learning much more effective; it also allowed us to adapt to changes and discuss the day's topics intelligently. Being prepared in the realm of customer service starts with a good understanding of how services differ from products, and thus how we can improve our knowledge and skills to deliver service that meets (at a minimum!) customer wants and needs. In this chapter we will show you how your preparation can make a significant positive impact on the customer's experience.

The Business of Services (versus Products)

As a services professional, your desire is to be prepared to provide excellent service, whatever the situation you find yourself and your customer in. To ensure both you and your employees are prepared to do so, you should first have everyone involved understand the general nature of a service-based business versus a product-based one.

While they are important for products as well, some variables that may take on even more significance in the service industry are trust, time, reliability, and relationships. The people factor is of monumental importance. With the ubiquitous nature of online shopping, you may or may not interact with a person. But in most cases with service, a person is vital. Thus, there is much more chance of human error. There are, of course, services that do not require a person (like your Internet connection, electric or gas utilities for your house, and the like). Of course if there is an interruption in the service, you want a person with whom you can talk. But a repair service, pest control, doctors, lawyers, etc., rely on the interaction with the service provider. And then businesses such as bridal shops, car rental dealerships, and restaurants involve service *and* a product.

As we have mentioned, organizations providing services face similar issues to those providing products regarding planning, management, marketing, and innovation. In your own experience, you have probably noticed that there are several notable *dissimilarities* as well! Researchers have documented, over a long period, many such differences in the marketing of products versus services. A service provider is the product. Thus, marketing a service means you need to instill trust and confidence in your abilities. Selling a service also means you are selling time. The customer expects you to deliver results within an agreed upon timeframe. Marketing a service means you must build a relationship. Remember the widely known "four Ps" in marketing products we described in the Introduction. An approach concerning the differences in marketing services isolates four of the most familiar differences, all of which begin with the letter "I" and thus give the concept its name, the "four Is of Services." These factors are *intangibility, inconsistency, inseparability*, and *inventory*. Let's look at each of these factors.

The Four Is of Service

Intangibility. While product purchase decisions can be based in part on the physical nature of the product being considered, the same is not true with services. Being intangible means that other ways must be used in place of actual examination of the product in advance of purchase. The goal for service providers is to "make the intangible tangible" as much as is possible in a consumer's mind.

Inconsistency. Production standards have long been a part of the production of physical products. If you make bottled juices, then taste, color, and the amount of juice in each bottle will vary very little whether you buy a bottle at a Kroger store in Lexington, Kentucky or at a convenience store in Lexington, Massachusetts. When you go to McDonald's, you expect your Big Mac to look and taste exactly the same in Las Vegas, Nevada as it does in Cincinnati, Ohio. Quality control and other operations management practices are in place to assure this. Services, on the other hand, tend to have greater variance in the quality level a customer receives. This can be because of the training and experience of a particular service provider, along with other environmental effects such as the number of customers or the time of day (just think of the service quality differences possible among the four cashiers involved in buying the juice or Big Macs). Even when machines provide a service, there can be variations from one time or place to another. Thus, the best service providers constantly seek to overcome inconsistency as much as is possible.

Inseparability. Judging a product's quality and consistency is easy. If two bottles of juice from the producer described above are bought in two different places and then compared, they should be nearly identical. When a customer experiences a service, on the other hand, it is difficult to separate the service from who or what is delivering that service. Thus, service providers are always looking for ways to avoid having a service delivery person or machine negatively affect the perception of the service itself.

Inventory. Products are made and then shipped to places where they are stored until sold, with many categories of goods going through several stages of transit and storage in a channel of distribution. Services cannot be stored. If your classroom holds 40 students and only 20 students enroll in a given class, then you cannot save the unused capacity. An airline with a flight from Nashville to Orlando that can seat 140 passengers but only books 120 cannot save the unused seats and sell them later (yes, even deeply discounted!).

Know How the Four Is Relate to Your Business

So what about your organization? How are you handling the four Is of service right now? To what degree are your offerings tangible versus intangible? Do all employees perform at the desired level 100% of the time? Do your employees enhance the customer's experience? Are you able to manage your demand to prevent lost business and lost opportunities? In short, are you prepared? Let's take a look.

Tangibles. Restaurant owners would answer that they have both tangible and intangible elements in their business. They're right, and many other types of service businesses do as well. In fact, there is a concept, the *service continuum*, which describes varying proportions of product versus service of particular market offerings. The closer a business comes to the "purely a service" side of the continuum, the more it should be prepared to fully address the four "Is."

Customers judge services on several fronts. One of the first impressions they form is based on how well your organization *appears* to be

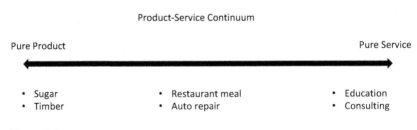

Figure 1.1

able to provide the service they want. This appearance will differ depending on what type of service you offer and whether it is attached to a product or is a pure service. Physical facilities need to be in good repair, not necessarily fancy, but they should appear to your customers that you are set up to enable the promised service to be delivered. For example, if you repair automobiles, your facility can look busy and not be as clean as would be expected if you were offering a dry cleaning service. If your service is delivered on the customer's premises, such as with windshield replacement or pest control services, the service person(s) should appear competent and prepared to do the job.

Terry's son and his wife had an interesting experience illustrating these effects, good and bad. They were driving in from Texas for a visit and had car trouble. Because the warranty was still in effect, they contacted Honda Roadside Assistance which arranged for a tow to the nearest dealership. When the driver arrived, they were a bit concerned. He was dressed shabbily and wore both a scruffy beard and a holstered pistol. His demeanor matched his look, as he cursed regularly and complained about how there were closer trucks that could have been called instead of him. He loaded up the car and the three of them entered the cab for the 80-mile trip. They soon discovered that there were no seatbelts and that the overall appearance of the tow truck was a good match for that of the driver. As they made their way to the dealership the driver talked lovingly about his truck, that he had been driving it for ten years, and that he had personally put over 300,000 miles on it.

They arrived at the dealership but it was late at night and the driver suggested that they drop the car and then he would take them to one of the nearby hotels. Thus, what looked to be a questionable event at first turned into an interesting couple of hours and expert, caring service. The driver's appearance (and that of his trusty truck) set up an

expectation of concern while the actual service was top-notch. However, you cannot count on your customers overlooking those tangibles associated with your particular type of business, so working to make them a part of your overall image and competence is the wiser way. That and perhaps a no-cursing policy.

For example, workers must have the parts and equipment necessary for carrying out various routine jobs. As you saw earlier in the chapter, one of the key differences in selling services versus products is that the latter are tangible in nature; one can see, inspect, and try out an item before purchase. Services, on the other hand, are intangible. Cues you offer the customer will help set expectations and determine, in part, how well you meet or exceed those expectations. Some of the basic ways to make the intangible tangible are:

- Uniforms for service personnel
- Testimonials from satisfied customers
- Promotional products, especially ones that are useful on a daily basis, such as calendars, drink coasters, and letter openers
- Your logo and other explanatory signage on vehicles, equipment, etc.

The first and last of these four methods are self-explanatory, and you are likely including them in your efforts already. Although testimonials are well understood too, it is important to note that you *must* keep them up-to-date on whatever media you use to disseminate them. If, for example, you no longer provide a particular service, but a customer is on record in a video on your website, or in a printed brochure, telling everyone how great that service is, you are sending customers a sign that you are not prepared. "What other little details might these people overlook?" a customer might think.

The third item, promotional products, is an often misunderstood, but potentially valuable, way to connect with customers. Used correctly, research shows that they can help keep a service provider's existence in front of the customer. The best such products are ones that can be left with or sent to a customer and that are useful for everyday tasks. The simplest items are inexpensive and yet have an impact that goes for months or years beyond a service encounter. These items should resonate with your particular type of business. If you own a restaurant, for example, you might distribute themed calendars with special dates and coupons on each month's page. Your restaurant customers (and catering customers, if you offer such an option) will see your name and logo, advertising messages, etc., multiple times each day. For example, Chick-fil-A has given away calendars with cute pictures and monthly promotions, complete with tear-off coupons. There is a reason a dry cleaner's address and other contact information are printed on the hangers holding its customers' clothing!

Inconsistency. To reduce inconsistent service delivery, make sure that your training prepares people to deliver, that any necessary certifications are kept up to date, and that you do not overwork service personnel so they are tired and just trying to get through the day so they can rest. Depending on the type of service involved, such rest is important to avoid safety failures, far more important than the delivery of service. Railroads and airlines are two industries where safety violations have caused unsafe conditions leading to accidents that then led to changes in company policies and regulations regarding crew rest. In Chapter 7 we present a valuable tool, the Gaps model, that can help overcome inconsistency, as well as inseparability.

Inseparability. If your type of service is one that is totally dependent on the service provider, i.e., the customer sees him or her as the service itself, then the other three "Is" become even more important. Designing a proper service delivery system, training your people on it, plus allowing them time to do their job correctly are all important in such settings. Lands' End is consistently at the top of customer service ratings, in part because each representative is given over 65 hours of training (Lands' End, n.d.). You can leverage your tangibles efforts here as well; customers who have your name, logo, and other evidence of where the service is coming from can help make sure you don't lose any of them if one of your employees moves to a competitor. In other words, you want to make sure customers associate the service with your business, not with specific employees.

Inventory. As we said above, services cannot be "stored." Thus, service companies have developed methods and practices to manage this "perishable" inventory. You are quite familiar with some of these approaches, such as the reduced prices airlines and restaurants use to shift demand to off-peak periods. Alternatively or in combination higher prices for peak demand periods can lead to customers choosing other times of the year (or day or time) to use the service. For your particular type of service, it is, of course, very important that any materials and equipment necessary for delivering it are on hand and readily accessible if a spike in demand appears unexpectedly.

The Fishbein Model

One tool you can use to help determine what to emphasize in your own service environment is the model commonly known as the Fishbein model (Fishbein, 1963). First, a little background. Martin Fishbein was a psychologist and a professor at the University of Illinois. He developed a series of models based on the premise that a person's attitude toward something could be broken down into attitudes toward the various attributes of which that thing was comprised (i.e., the whole *is* the sum of the parts!). This is the reason the descriptive name includes "multi-attribute." Some of these attributes are considered to be more important than others and thus these models include an importance weight for each attribute. Besides the thing or things being considered, the list of attributes comprising it/them, and how important each attribute is, a fourth and final part needed to build the model is what Fishbein termed "beliefs." Equivalent terms for beliefs would include words like "ratings" and "performance scores."

This flexible model can be applied in practically any situation for nearly any type of task. It is in the class of models known as "compensatory" models, because it allows strengths to compensate for weaknesses. (A rather unwieldy other name for it is the multi-attribute decision-making model.) You can easily design a customized Fishbein model for your particular application, enter appropriate data, and interpret the results. Regardless of what you call it, any business owner or manager should know how to use this tool, and we believe you will find it a valuable asset for improving customer service.

At the end of the chapter, you will have an opportunity to design a model to see how it is done. For now, let's look at a completed model and learn the basic components that comprise it. The model below compares three providers of lawn care services on three typical characteristics.

Table 1.1 Lawn Care Companies

Attribute	Importance	BeGreen	GreenIt	UrLawn
Speed	0.2	4	3	3
Accuracy	0.5	3	5	4
Price	0.3	5	4	3
		3.8	4.3	3.5

Let's say the data in the model was generated from surveys among 100 customers.

The numbers in the model are the average ratings from these customers in two areas: (1) how important each characteristic (in the language of such models these are known as "attributes") is in the evaluation of lawn care services and (2) how each provider was rated on its performance for each attribute. The most common approach to rating attribute importance is as a proportion of 1. So, price is rated as a moderately important factor of 3, and accuracy is the most important factor with its rating of 5. Of least importance is speed at 2. For performance on these attributes, the table of numbers (which are termed "beliefs" in the language of Fishbein models) shows how customers rated them. The model is calculated by multiplying the attribute weight and the rating for each attribute for each provider.

Thus, the model has four parts – the things being compared, the attributes that comprise them, how important the attributes are in making a decision, and how each item performed on each attribute. The model's results appear below each entity in the model. Here, GreenIt has come out on top as the best lawn care provider. Remember, this is the result for these three brands for these 100 customers and these three attributes. Changing any of these factors will change the results. The most valuable aspect of Fishbein models is the diagnostic options for use in decisions regarding the items that were compared in a given model. Here, let's look at the results for each provider as if we are a manager for a given firm.

As we said above, GreenIt is the overall "winner" in our fictional customer survey. GreenIt could state this fact in various promotional efforts. You have likely seen comparative ads in a magazine that tout the advertised brand against two competing brands. If the ad is to be believed by the target market, it should be based on some type of empirical research such as we presented above. In fact, that type of fact is usually stated in a footnote in the ad itself. Some such ads show a table with a check mark or star or some other symbol next to the attributes, with the advertised brand having more such positive marks versus its competitors.

Besides such a use for the overall results, Fishbein models also provide multiple opportunities for diagnostic evaluations and competitive decisions. For example, one common use is to focus on attributes that are important to customers and for which you are behind one or more competitors. The model helps you focus on such areas to get the most out of improvement investments. Here, BeGreen and UrLawn should investigate ways to complete their services in a more accurate manner. Companies may also discover that other attributes on which they are the best are not being considered in a particular model; simply making customers aware of that attribute and your performance on it can shift overall model results more in your favor.

Once you begin putting the model to use you will be able to see many applications for it to help you be prepared for your service roles. For example, you can compare your own organization to other units in your company or to similar competitor organizations. In Chapter 7 we will present a service improvement model for which Fishbein models can supply data.

Apply Rule #1: Come to Class Prepared

Know the four Is of service and how they relate to your business. Be prepared to meet and exceed customer expectations.

1   How are your employees prepared and equipped to provide great service? How might you improve such preparation and equip them even better? Ask them to discuss these aspects of their jobs during your next meeting or training session.
2   What types of tangibles are you using now? Think of three additional ways you can "make the intangible tangible." Use competitors or excellent service providers from your own experience, even those in different lines of business.
3   Create a Fishbein model for your business and two of your competitors, preferably your strongest ones. Information for your model might be from your own knowledge, expertise, and experience. It could also come from your employees or outside sources, such as surveys, industry sources, trade association studies, chamber of commerce data. Templates are available on our website, simplecustomerservicerules.com, under Resources.

References

Fishbein, M. (1963). An investigation of the relationships between beliefs about an object and attitude toward the object. *Human Relation, 16,* 233–240.

Lands' End (n.d.). *About Us.* https://www.landsend.com/aboutus/values/. Accessed 04/11/18

2

COMPLETE ASSIGNMENTS
NEATLY AND ON TIME

"A little too late, is much too late." – German Proverb

In school, completing assignments on time showed that we were reliable. Being timely demonstrated that we were responsive to the expectations. For instance, if an essay on "What I did during the summer" is due on Monday, September 9, the teacher expects to have it in class on that day.

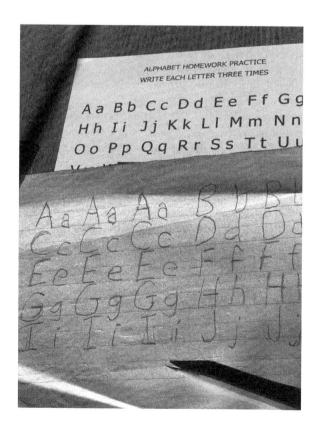

Even in kindergarten, we might have been given a worksheet to practice writing the alphabet over the weekend. We would be expected to have that worksheet complete when we came to class on Monday. Timeliness assured our teacher that we were making appropriate effort. These are the same things customers expect from the organizations with which they interact. Customers expect responsiveness in a timely manner.

In their book, *Delivering Service Quality*, Zeithaml, Parasuraman, and Berry (1990) show that the two most important aspects of service, from the customer's perspective, are **reliability** and **responsiveness**. The rule of completing assignments neatly and on time is directly related to these so-called *service dimensions*. In their decades of published research on measuring and improving service delivery, Zeithaml and her colleagues set the standard for modern-day study of services.

Let's look at how these two key service elements relate to being neat and on time.

Reliability

Zeithaml et al. describe *reliability* as the service provider's ability to perform a service dependably and accurately. This is generally the single most important service dimension, as people seeking a service want that service done, and done right. This means the service must at least *meet* customer expectations. To be good at customer service, you must know your customers' expectations; in fact, *you are responsible for setting them!* What is the minimum requirement? What should the gold standard be?

These expectations serve as the foundation for communication with the customer. Thus, setting expectations is a necessity; it is of key importance to do this in advance of the service delivery, so that you are always meeting those expectations, and in some cases exceeding them. If your service personnel don't have, say, uniforms as nice as those of your competitors but your people deliver what you said they would every single time, then your service satisfaction ratings will be better than those competitors who look the part but don't play it that well.

Consider an experience Ed had at the post office.

> *I ordered a custom hand-made ring for a special occasion for a family member. The jeweler lives in Taiwan, so I figured it might take a while to arrive at my home in the United States once it was sent from Taiwan. When it hadn't arrived two months after it had been sent, though, I contacted the jeweler in Taiwan to see what might have happened to delay it. He gave me a tracking number. Once I followed the trail, I discovered that the ring had actually been sitting at my branch of the post office for a month! I couldn't believe it! An employee had checked it in, but*

20

had never sent it out for delivery or sent notification to me sot that I could go pick it up. If I hadn't tracked it down myself, it would have been returned to Taiwan, simply because the postal worker had not done his or her job.

A few months after this experience, I was in the main post office branch downtown. I needed to get my passport picture taken. The department that provided that service was upstairs in the building and opened at 9:00am. It was only 8:50am, but I went upstairs to the office anyway, expecting to wait until 9:00. Although I was in a hurry to get to a meeting, I figured I could spare the 10 minutes. However, the postal worker saw me and graciously let me in and took my picture. Everything was complete before 9:00am when the office actually opened! She then walked me downstairs and retrieved a copy of the official form and an addressed envelope for me so that completing the application would go more quickly. When I went back a couple of days later to mail the package, this same employee looked over it for me to make sure I had completed the form properly.

Back downstairs at the counter, as I paid for the photo and some stamps, I half-jokingly said that this branch should do customer service training for the branch in my neighborhood. (I have always had a pleasant experience at the main branch and rarely have had what I would consider a good experience at my neighborhood branch.) The woman who was serving me replied, "I used to work at that branch. I put in for a transfer." She went on to say that there was really only one nice person at the other branch. She said that she knew it shouldn't be that *way, but the environment at the other branch impacted how postal workers treated customers as well. At this main office, everyone was nice. It was a much more pleasant environment in which to work.*

Because the culture at the main branch was more positive and the employees enjoyed being around one another, they felt better about themselves and their environment; in turn, they were nicer to customers. Consequently, the customers had a better experience and were nicer in return, thus continuing the cycle.

This difference in culture meant the postal workers cared more about their job and were more reliable. Before purchasing his current house, Ed and his family had a P.O. box at this main branch. It is not very likely that Ed's package would have sat at the main branch for a month had that been its final destination. In fact, the package did have to pass through the main branch before reaching its final destination where it ended up sitting for the month. According to the tracking information, it was only at the main branch for a few hours before being sent on to the destination branch.

Why did Ed travel several miles further to go to the main branch to complete his passport application? He went there in part because they were more pleasant, but mostly because they were more reliable and dependable.

Responsiveness

Among the other service dimensions, research has found that *responsiveness* is seen as second in importance only to reliability. Responsiveness means being prompt in doing what you said you'd do. (That is, it goes hand in hand with reliability.) In the post office example, the main office was much more responsive than the local branch. In fact, when Ed called about his package after finally tracking it down, it took several additional phone calls and a trip to the final destination branch (including a half hour wait in line) to get a package that should have been delivered weeks earlier. Why didn't the post office deliver the package after the error was brought to their attention? Why did it take several days just to get a call back on the initial inquiry? After finding out that the package had already been there for a month, that didn't seem very prompt to Ed, but a few additional days of delay after all that time that the package had been sitting at the branch probably seemed prompt to the postal workers.

"Promptly" is one of those words with a different meaning to different people. The key again is to set expectations. If you know your schedule is such that it allows you to get to a customer and do the job within two days *maximum*, then promise that. If you never go past the maximum then you'll build a good reputation for being responsive. For those times you will be able to perform the service in a timeframe less than the maximum, then your customers will see it as exceeding their expectations. (When Ed went to the upstairs department at the post office to get his passport photo ten minutes before the stated opening time, that postal worker exceeded his expectation when she not only let him in, but also immediately attended to his needs. Ed saw the sign with the hours of operation and had expected to wait the ten minutes until opening time. He was pleasantly surprised by the unexpected service effort.)

It is possible a salesperson, for instance, might lose a sale or two because another company's sales representative promises product delivery much sooner, even though he or she *knows* it will not be possible to deliver the order on time. It will be after the fact that the customer realizes the better option would have been to go with the more realistic salesperson. Not delivering as promised will eventually impact the second salesperson's sales because customers will begin to realize they can rely on the first salesperson and will trust him or her in the future. Here, in trying to "overdo" responsiveness, reliability is affected. However, high levels of both are needed to excel in customer service.

For years, we have run a simple exercise in our classes and at meetings to demonstrate how we all understand words representing time and probability a little (and sometimes a lot!) differently. The exercise itself is explained fully in the appendix. Participating in the exercise demonstrates how varied our understanding of time and probability words are. These are simple words and simple concepts, so what could go wrong? The answer is plenty! Following is an overview of the gist, but we encourage you to read about the exercise and how to conduct it in the appendix.

Our research has shown how two different parties can misinterpret the type of everyday language used in service interactions of all kinds. The resulting miscommunication can defeat systems that were designed to deliver service reliably and promptly. Let's take a look at how this can occur and how you can help your organization prevent it.

Miscommunication is a Problem for Customer Service

When you hear someone tell you that something will "probably" happen, what does *probably* mean to you? That is, if you were to put an actual probability in place of that word, what number would you use? 80%? 67%? Our research (Holmes and Brewer, 2006; Brewer and Holmes, 2009; Brewer and Holmes, 2016) shows that the word *probably* is interpreted to mean about 65%, on average. However, the range we have found in our research is from less than 50% to over 90%! Thus, an average is not the best statistic to use when you are trying to communicate accurately. That average from our research results is based on *hundreds* of responses, but stop here for a moment and ask yourself this question: what matters most for two people trying to reach an understanding through communication? It is how closely the actual probabilities each person defines the terms to mean line up, and, most importantly, whether they are aware of any difference.

Consider the following scenario. A customer calls one of your employees and asks if a special order has been delivered yet. Your employee may look it up and see that it is due to arrive in tomorrow's delivery from that vendor. However, he also knows that the vendor has been hit with some performance problems recently, so there is a 50% chance that it will be a day late, and a much smaller chance of being two or three days late. Taking all of this into consideration, he tells the customer, "It should be in soon, probably today or tomorrow." (Notice he has now combined probability and time in his statement.) Let's say if he were asked that his response to the question of what "probably" means would be close to the 65% average we have found. Unfortunately, given that she just heard that the order "should be in *soon, probably* tomorrow," your customer (being a "probably" = 90% kind of person) plans to take off work tomorrow morning to make the 50-mile trip to pick up the order. Imagine for a moment the scene when she arrives and is told that the product is not there!

This type of miscommunication is widespread and not limited to just this word, or even a few others. *Probably* is just one of many words that are tossed around casually, without thought to an actual meaning until a misunderstanding has already occurred and hurt feelings, anger, and dissatisfaction all follow. In fact, the exercise used as part of our miscommunication research features four other such terms related to probability. We have learned from our students, clients, and colleagues of many other problematic words as well.

If the above scenario concerning the use of the term "probably" seems like an easy thing to fix, consider also that there is another aspect to such miscommunication – time-related terms. You may have noticed three of these terms, *soon, today,* and *tomorrow,* were used in the example above. Brace yourself, because our research shows that these particular words are *also* interpreted with widely ranging meaning. "Soon" means about eight hours on average, but has a range of responses from less than an hour all the way to *more than one week*! Even the seemingly self-descriptive words "today" and "tomorrow" vary depending on context and time of day they are used.

Participants in our research exercise have reported how widespread these types of miscommunication events are. They have shared with us some of the ways people have tried to combat the resulting problems in their workplaces. These range from the humorous approach of a plant manager literally banning the use of the term "ASAP" from all e-mail

correspondence to the much more reasonable, and effective, training of personnel to communicate more clearly. Below, we offer lessons to learn to help avoid this common type of miscommunication. Though of course these will not *eliminate* miscommunication, they can raise awareness among employees that will contribute to fewer instances of it. The end result will be better customer service through improved reliability and responsiveness.

Communication Exercise Lessons

1 Use clear language ("by lunch" instead of "soon")
2 State deadlines clearly and specifically ("tomorrow at 10:00 a.m." instead of "tomorrow")
3 Ask questions to clarify mutual understanding

It seems to us that part of the problem is that there simply is not pride in one's work across any given organization. Almost three decades ago, Leonard Schlesinger and James Heskett (1991) addressed this issue in an article titled "Breaking the Cycle of Failure in Services." Unfortunately, the cycle has not been broken. Workers are still often paid minimally, and do minimal work. We bet you have heard, as we have, a cashier at a grocery or retail store, say something to the effect of, "only 20 more minutes until my shift is over!" If they haven't said it out loud, you might be able to tell by their nonverbal interactions. Their heart isn't in it; they appear ready to go home. If the customer experiences this lack of attention, do you suppose they feel good about the service they are receiving? (Instead of a store cashier, what if it was your bank loan officer, mechanic, or doctor with this attitude?) It is not always possible to offer more money to employees to make them more motivated. But it is not always money that makes the difference! The postal worker in Ed's story asked to be transferred to a different branch, not because of the promise of more money, but because of an environment that was more enjoyable. Customer service improved not because of money but because of the environment in which it was being delivered. The lessons of being more reliable and responsive to your customers can help you improve the environment in your organization.

Apply Rule #2: Complete Assignments Neatly and on Time

Be Reliable and Responsive

1   How do you keep track of your service reliability now? How frequently do you collect data? How do you share it with your employees? Is it used in your training for current and new employees?

   Possibilities:
   Percentage of deliveries on time, early, and late
   Percentage of returns
   Number of customer complaint calls

2   How quickly does your organization respond to inquiries? From phone calls to social media messages, from e-mails to physical letters, you need to know what your response time averages for every aspect of your customer service operations. This is true for both external customers and fellow workers in various areas of your business.

   Possibilities:
   Call logs

Service journals
Customer inquiries
Surveys
Secret Shoppers
How does your response time compare to your competitors or to
   industry averages?

3   Run the communication exercise with eight to ten of your employ-
    ees. (Complete Instructions are in the appendix.) Depending on
    how many employees you have this could be done within your man-
    agement team, within a unit with its supervisor and employees, or
    with any other combination of your people. You will bring to light
    how easily miscommunication can lead to difficulties and unhappy
    customers.

References

Brewer, E. C., and Holmes, T. L. (2009). Obfuscating the obvious: Miscommunication issues in the interpretation of common terms. *Journal of Business
   Communication, 46*, 480–496.
Brewer, E. C., and Holmes, T. L. (2016). Better communication = better teams:
   A communication exercise to improve team performance. *IEEE Transactions
   on Professional Communication, 59*(3), 288–298.
Holmes, T. L., and Brewer E. C. (May 2006). An experiential classroom exercise to improve communication effectiveness. *The Archive of Marketing Education.* http://www.Marketingpower.com in the academic section
Schlesinger, L. A., and Heskett, James, L. (Spring 1991). Breaking the cycle of
   failure in services. *MIT Sloan Management Review.* https://sloanreview.mit.
   edu/article/breaking-the-cycle-of-failure-in-services/
Zeithaml, Valarie A., Parasuraman, A., and Berry, Leonard L. (1990). *Delivering quality service: Balancing customer perception and expectation.* New
   York: The Free Press, A Division of Simon & Shuster, Inc.

3

PAY ATTENTION

"If there is any one secret of success, it lies in the ability to get the other person's point of view and see things from that person's angle as well as from your own." – Henry Ford

Whether as a child in kindergarten or as a professional in a required continuing education seminar, when we pay attention in class, we learn better. This is true in providing world-class customer service as well. When you pay attention in customer interactions, you can learn about his or her needs and then prepare to respond appropriately. What do we need to do in order to pay attention? We need to listen. Listening is not simply hearing. Listening is taking that information and processing it to store it and to make it useful.

Listening and Understanding Needs

Listen to what your customer is saying. Ask questions. Some people are afraid to speak when listening to someone, thinking it would be rude to interrupt. Even if not interrupting, the train of thought can cause you to wait until the other person has run out of words. This approach is not good for clear communication. Rather, active listening involves you talking as well. So, you can sometimes find solutions to problems by understanding what the customer really wants.

For example, what a customer says and what a customer actually wants are not always exactly the same. Let's say a customer purchases a red espresso machine from a retail store. She gets it home and sets in on the counter, and it just doesn't look right. She plugs it in but does not actually use it. Even though she knows that it would work quite well, somehow it just doesn't seem right in her kitchen. She takes it back to the store and asks for a refund. What this customer really wants, even if she doesn't realize it yet, is to exchange the red machine for a black one. If the store employee were to ask some questions, and then listen to the

customer actively, he might discover this and save the sale. By listening, and paying attention to the customer and her needs, we can help get to the real issue that the customer herself might not realize.

When we were small children, our parents and teachers told us to "sit up straight; don't slouch." These simple nonverbal actions can indicate we are listening. The same holds true for the words many of us heard in our youth: "Look at me when I talk to you." If we are not looking at the customer (at least in American culture), it may appear that we are not paying attention to what they are saying. This can especially be a problem today with all the ever-present distractions (smart phones, etc.). We may actually be looking on our computer or hand-held device screen seeking an answer to help him, but to the customer it could appear that we are not paying attention. Also, paying attention gives us a chance to offer empathy to our customer. We will address empathy a little later.

Listening as a Signal of Service

Besides enabling you to understand a particular customer's needs better, active listening signals the customer as to the service they can expect as well. Our earlier discussion of service dimensions applies here as well. Asking questions (as long as you do so during natural places in the conversation) shows that you are listening and that you are seeking clarification so that the best possible service can result.

Ed recalls a morning when he did not receive his newspaper. He called the newspaper office to report it. First, he called the local number and got a recording that the number was no longer in service and to call the 1–800 number. He then did call the 1–800 phone number and was referred, by a recorded message, back to the first number. When he finally reached an active number, he was led through a series of prompts, either speaking a word or pushing a number on his phone. He was never actually able to talk to a person, and once he was through the system, he received a message that he had been credited for the paper. *But that's not what he wanted!* He wanted an actual paper for the day. There was, however, *no option in the series of prompts to find out what he really wanted.* (Incidentally, Ed also never actually received credit for the missing paper and several additional papers have been missing.)

Listening can signal the customer that we understand his or her needs and will make adjustments to provide the proper service. In today's world of automation, there is a lack of person-to-person contact. If you want to provide excellent customer service and are using automation, you need to discover ways to actually listen. Perhaps this means always having an option to talk to a customer service agent if the automated prompts are not able to meet customer needs. When the automation works for the customer, it can be quicker and leave the customer satisfied. However, when it doesn't work, as in Ed's example, having the opportunity to talk to a knowledgeable customer service agent could make all the difference between a satisfied or unsatisfied customer.

Listening and responding is part of active listening and shows the customer not only that you are paying attention to their description but that you are a professional who is alert and ready to work on their problem.

Ed's mother decided to cancel her membership with a service provider she had been with for more than 60 years. The customer service agent's response upon hearing the request to cancel was simply "OK" and to give her the necessary procedure to cancel her account. How would you feel if this happened to you? Does 60 years of patronage not mean anything? What could the customer service agent have done in this case instead of, or at least in addition to, simply deleting the long-time customer's account? First, she could have said something like, "I am sorry you want to cancel your service." Then she might have followed up with, "May I ask why you want to cancel after all of these years" or "Is there a problem with the service?" Had she taken this approach in this case, she would have discovered it was purely a financial issue. Ed's mom was seeking to reduce expenses. Perhaps there is something she could have done to lower the cost to keep the customer.

Maybe she couldn't have kept this customer, but at least she would have valued her. The customer might then still leave, but with a positive feeling about the company, and perhaps the positive word of mouth that would accompany that feeling. As it ended in this case, the customer left feeling hurt and angry that after 60 years of patronage all she got was "OK." The customer service agent wasn't alert to what her customer was saying. This scenario, of course, also ties in with the idea of expressing empathy.

Empathy

Depending on the service(s) you offer, such empathy is needed from time to time, if not always. Repair services are sought, sometimes on an emergency basis, because equipment has broken, leaving the customer without the benefit of whatever that equipment had been doing. From losing air conditioning in a retail business to having a teenage son drive through a closed garage door, the customer is sometimes having a very bad day and is depending on you (whether or not they actually say it) not only to correct the problem but also to lend a sympathetic ear.

Please note that empathy is not the same as sympathy. It is also not necessarily agreeing with the customer. Empathy simply means understanding – understanding where the customer is coming from and what they are feeling – and ensuring him or her that you know/understand this. Done correctly, the customer realizes the person opposite

them is ready to act on their behalf. It is out of empathy that we can offer meaningful solutions.

Let's look at an example. Say a customer's air conditioning goes out in the middle of July, in Florida. He calls Comfort Air Heating and Cooling, which is swamped with other work orders. It could be an entire week before his repair can be started. Simply telling the customer this is not going to make him happy; also, it doesn't demonstrate any empathy at all. Perhaps Comfort Air could loan the customer a window air conditioner until they can get to the repair. This option probably wouldn't cool the entire house, but it could provide for a room or two to be moderately comfortable. There are countless other ways, of course, to demonstrate empathy. The main point is that it is important to demonstrate to the customer that *you care and understand their situation*, even if you can't fix it right away. This subtle approach could make all the difference in the customer's attitude toward the entire Comfort company, not just its service and repair side.

Look at Me When I Talk to You

Though we have mentioned this earlier, it bears repeating here. Eye contact is important, at least in the United States. Have you ever watched a parent or a teacher trying to explain something to or discipline a child while the child seems utterly distracted, looking everywhere but at the person who is talking to them? How do you think that parent or teacher feels? How do you suppose a customer feels if the customer service agent (salesperson, cashier, service writer, etc.) is not looking at them while they talk? Eye contact is another way to convey confidence and show you are listening. This relates to the importance of nonverbal interactions

that we have discussed as well, with eye contact alone sometimes being enough to relate that you understand and will use what you're hearing to help you deliver what the customer needs. We discuss some nonverbal issues throughout the book. Being aware of what you are projecting to the customer is important.

Perception

Our perception of what is happening in an interaction and the customer's perception do not always line up. We need to look at our interactions from the customer's perception. If a customer purchases a $30,000 vehicle with a 3-year/36,000-mile warranty and the transmission fails at 37,000 miles, the dealer may see it as simply out of warranty. The customer may think a car should last longer than 37,000 miles before having a significant problem. Perhaps this customer is a salesperson who travels a lot and put this 37,000 on his car in 11 months. Now, not only do you have a customer who thinks a $30,000 car should last longer than 37,000 miles, but she is also upset because the car is not even a year old yet.

Perception goes beyond the above scenario. Consider that a $30,000 car is a lot of money for one customer, but to a customer who is seeking to purchase a $440,000 Rolls Royce Phantom Coupe, $30,000 may not even be the down payment (if such a customer even needs a down payment!). For someone who lives in Phoenix, Arizona, 80 degrees in mid-July would be a cool day, but in Anchorage, Alaska, that 80 degrees in mid-July would be sweltering. In November, a 40-degree day in Anchorage would be quite warm, but in Phoenix would be unpleasantly cold. Perception is important. Understanding a customer's perception will help you better meet his or her needs. Even in those cases when you cannot satisfy a customer, your understanding will help you to explain why you cannot in a way that will make sense to him or her. He or she may not be happy, but at least you can prevent him or her from being angry. The Fishbein model we discussed earlier was originally designed as a way to measure, understand, and then try to change attitudes. It can be applied in many ways as you seek to measure, understand, and try to set your customers' expectations about your service.

What do your customers think about your brand? Your business is built on your customer relationships and how your customers perceive your brand. Consumers today share information on Facebook, Twitter, Instagram, Pinterest, and all other kinds of social media. It doesn't matter if *you* think you are giving good service, it is the *customer's* perception that impacts the image of your brand. Paying attention by monitoring and understanding customer perception is vital. You can change the way your customers feel about you for the better by following the simple rules in this book.

Nonverbals

We mention nonverbal interactions throughout this book because such interactions are so very important. We tend not to pay attention to our *own* nonverbals . . . and this can be disastrous. Just because *we* think we have a smile on our face or look happy does not mean our customers perceive it that way. We should take some time to discuss nonverbal communication with our coworkers, and we should watch for situations in which customers may be misinterpreting nonverbal interactions, so that we can adjust them accordingly.

Other nonverbal elements can either add to the overall effect of a professional service provider working hard to get all the information possible or completely destroy it in the time it takes to yawn. Checking your phone, even if you are simply noting the time available and deciding how best to use it to help the customer can be misinterpreted as impatience. Worse, the customer may sense that you don't think her problem is worth your time and that you are really anticipating a more important meeting after this. Clothing and accessories are nonverbal. Proper attire can impact customer perception of your competence and your sincerity. Some organizations have dress codes because they are seeking to project a certain image.

In an article discussing research concerning nonverbal cues in service encounters, the impact of these nonverbal cues is explained:

> We find that the expressive similarity established at the start of a service encounter can potentially influence customer responses later in the customer experience (i.e., customer satisfaction, voice behavior, responses to service recovery efforts). Therefore, the initial customer-employee interaction is a key customer touch point that should be carefully managed.
>
> (Lim, Lee, and Foo, 2017, p. 673)

It is also important to pay attention to the nonverbal interactions of your customers. You can tell whether they are angry or not. You can tell if they are pleased with what you are saying or annoyed. You can tell if they are in a good mood or not. You can tell if they are really listening to what you are telling them or not. This is all information that can help you make adjustments to be able to better connect with your customer. Remember the story of the tow truck driver in Chapter 1? The driver was dressed shabbily and wore a pistol. He was grouchy, cursed a lot, and complained during most of the trip. The truck was run down, its seat belts removed. It eventually became clear that he was good at his job and cared about his customers. However, a different customer may have panicked and refused the tow, thus never realizing any of the positive aspects displayed later.

Apply Rule #3: Pay attention

Listen. Demonstrate empathy. Be aware of your nonverbal signals and the customer's nonverbal signals.

1   Improving listening skills can be incorporated into your employee training. Try the Active Listening Exercise in the appendix. You can also see a version of this on our website: simplecustomerservicerules. com, under Resources.

    Discuss how participants felt during the exercise and how this informs their understanding of customer service.

2   Develop a script for training employees to be aware of nonverbal aspects of communication and how customers might perceive them. Have employees list all the steps involved in a service call, from greeting upon arrival to summarizing the service and departing. Are there areas where a misperception of aloofness, uncaring demeanor, etc., could occur? Brainstorm with employees on ideas for how to counter any that the exercise detects. Compare with customer comments collected via a suggestion box, website, or social media accounts.

3   An exercise on selective attention can be found on our website: simplecustomerservicerules.com, under Resources. Preview it before using with your group (be sure not to give away the ending!) and discuss the results.

Reference

Lim, E., Lee, Y., and Foo, M. (2017). Frontline employees' nonverbal cues in service encounters: A double-edged sword. *Journal of the Academy of Marketing Science*, 45(5), 657–676. doi:10.1007/s11747-016-0479-4

4

SHOW RESPECT

"Without feelings of respect, what is there to distinguish men from beasts?" – Confucius

Paying attention and listening are certainly related and linked to respect. We show respect when we pay attention to others and when we treat them with regard. When you were young, you probably had a teacher or parent say to you, "don't talk with your mouth full." Of course there

is a visual aspect of talking with our mouth full that can be . . . . well, disgusting. But it is more than that. When our mouth is full we are likely mumbling, which makes us difficult to understand.

Another aspect of showing respect is telling the truth, being honest. There is a link here too, to the aspect of listening that involves looking at the person with whom we are communicating. This isn't always possible, as when we are online or on the phone, but we can do other things within a particular medium to indicate we are paying attention and respecting the customer. For example, a recent trend is that some businesses have begun offering to take callers' phone numbers and call or text them back instead of making them wait until the "next available agent." This has been well-received by customers because it is a sign of respect for the customer. We all desire respect.

Consider this story from Ed.

> *Much of my adult life I have owned a truck. I am often asked to help someone move something because of this vehicle preference. One time a friend, "Julian," asked if I could bring my truck to help move some furniture. Another friend, "Daryl," was also going to help with the effort, and we all planned to meet at my home at 7:00 a.m. Since my wife had worked late the previous night and we had a baby at home, I waited outside for my friends, so no one would ring the bell or knock on the door and wake up my wife and baby. At 7:15 am, Daryl finally showed up. He waited a few minutes, then left for coffee and returned. Finally, around 7:45 Julian, the person we were to help move, arrived. Neither friend expressed any chagrin at having me up early and waiting. In another such incident, I was asked to go to Julian's home to help pick up an item from a store that was too big for his car. I knocked on his door at the designated time only to find Julian and his wife just sitting down for dinner. I was offered a chair in the living room and sat there until they had finished and Julian told me he was ready to go.*

Whether it was a case of being preoccupied with the task at hand or simple cluelessness, the effect in both of these experiences was Ed having negative feelings from disrespect. Julian appeared to place more value on his own time, even if it wasn't mean-spirited or intentional. In business, keeping a customer on hold for a long time or giving them the runaround on the phone shows disrespect as well. Remember Ed trying to have his missing newspaper replaced? Does a series of automated voice commands, button pushing, call disconnections leave the customer feeling respected? Of course not!

Technology has had a huge impact on how we view customer service. We think that a personal human touch to interactions can make a tremendous difference in the customer's experience. Having positive human interaction can show the customer respect. Ed enjoys going to his Credit Union where they greet him by name and talk to him about things besides the financial transaction (a recent event, a holiday, family, the weather, etc.)

Because so much of our customer service is done technologically, it is important to examine how the customer and technology are interacting. Usability testing is a way to see how easy something is to use or understand. Typically, users are asked to complete tasks, while being observed to see if they encounter problems, what works well, etc. Developers often use this approach in designing a new website. This gives direct input into how real users experience and feel about the system. Why is this important? Why do we mention it here? Because it relates to what we have been talking about throughout this book. To offer great customer service, it is vital for you to know what customers are experiencing – to discover where they are having trouble, to learn how they *are* satisfied, and to find out how they are *not* satisfied.

Don't Talk with Your Mouth Full

This is a basic rule of good table manners. It also applies to respect in offering excellent customer service. When speaking, it is disrespectful to do so while eating or drinking so that you are not being as clear as possible. Previously, we discussed appearing distracted in the eyes of your customer. Looking at the clock or your watch could be seen as not respecting them and that someone or something must be more important to you.

With multitasking, there is not just a *perception* of this problem, *research shows it can be an actual detriment to performance and productivity.*

Multitasking is like talking with our mouth full. In their book *iBrain: Surviving the Technological Alteration of the Modern Mind*, Gary Small and Gigi Vorgan (2008) explain the problem with multitasking:

> Though we think we can get more done when we divide our attention and multitask, we are not necessarily more efficient. Studies show that when our brains switch back and forth from one task to another, our neural circuits take a small break in between. This is a time-consuming process that reduces efficiency. It's not unlike closing down one computer program and booting up another—it takes a few moments to shut down and start up. With each attention shift, the frontal lobe executive centers must activate different neural circuits (p. 68).

Thus, when we are on the computer or on the phone while talking with a customer face-to-face, even if we are looking up information to try to address their issue, we cannot help but to be distracted. Our attention is even more divided if we are trying to text our friend about plans for that evening while addressing the customer's needs.

In the technology-intensive world in which we live, multitasking is commonplace. We may even feel that we aren't being efficient if we aren't multitasking. But just because we *can* multitask and maybe even appear good at multitasking, doesn't mean we are *actually* good at it. This is because we cannot give our full attention to more than one item at a time. "Digital natives" (who, according to Small and Vorgan, are those who have grown up with technology) can often handle three or even more tasks simultaneously, while "digital immigrants" (who, according to Small and Vorgan, are those who came to the digital computer age as adults) prefer and usually function better with one task at a time.

But remember, just because digital natives can handle multiple tasks at one time does not mean that they are good at it either! As Small and Vorgan (2008) suggest:

> The truth is that everyone is somewhat challenged by multitasking. A recent UCLA experiment showed that when volunteers between eighteen and forty-five years old were given a learning task while being asked to keep a count of distracting beep sounds, their recall scores dropped dramatically in comparison with their performance when they were not distracted (p. 34).

So, to show respect, focus only on the customer at hand. Don't try to also help another customer at the same time or try to continue working on another task.

Tell the Truth – Honesty

When we were children, whether in kindergarten or at home, most of us were told to tell the truth. Some of us discovered that if we started to stretch the truth or tell "white lies," that it was easy to slide into more blatant untruths. We also may have discovered that it is hard to keep track of untruths (what exactly did I tell her?) and they can often come back to haunt us in some way. Being truthful is a part of showing respect to the customers in a service setting. Consider the following experience Terry and his family had at a local radio station's music festival:

Country Music Festival 2017

My daughter saw an online Father's Day promotion for a $5 per ticket discount for a three-artist music festival sponsored by a local country music station. She ordered three tickets at $20 each, plus the online ordering fees that applied. Thus the total was about $67.

When the day for the concert arrived, we printed our tickets to enable us to exchange them for the required wristbands at the venue gate that evening. As we stood in line to do so, we noticed that station personnel had tickets outside the gate area for $20 each, with no fees. Even more amazing was that those who were arriving got their wristbands from roving station staff; and then walked right past those who'd bought online and were waiting to obtain wristbands. Also, the station had advertised a 5:30 pm start time, even including that information on the online tickets, but the gates were actually set to open at 6:30, with no bathrooms outside the gates for the growing crowd to use. It was late June in western Tennessee, with the temperature near 90 degrees and the heat index even higher. We began to ask station staff who were selling the tickets if we might talk to someone about a refund, but each time the staff member passed the buck, claiming ignorance.

A young staffer finally summoned one of the station's on-air personalities. We again asked about a refund, but he stated that nobody with that authority was on site. After we finally made it to the ticket window and exchanged our tickets for wristbands, we asked another person wearing one of the station's yellow "Staff" shirts about a refund. She stated that she was the station's General Manager. We immediately knew that the on-air personality we had talked to just ten minutes earlier had actually lied to us, as he undoubtedly knew the person in overall charge of all station staff—his direct supervisor—was just fifty feet away.

The GM would not agree to a refund either. When we pointed out the experience we had gone through to that point, she was not sympathetic. Instead, she related that, earlier in her career, she had worked at a different music festival in the region that charged an even higher online premium versus the event's gate price! She then literally argued further with us and other station staff members began saying aloud that we were welcome to leave. However, the opening artist was a childhood friend of our daughter and so we decided to stay for her performance. It was a comedy of errors, though "tragedy of errors" would be more accurate!

Imagine one of your service providers, or anyone working in any position for you, actually lying to a customer. The loss of business you would face would likely not be limited to that one person or firm!

This more malicious form of dishonesty Terry experienced is hopefully rare, but employees often have other reasons for telling customers something that is untrue. In some instances, in their own minds, employees simply do not want to disappoint the customer right there on the spot. Perhaps they are hoping that they can find a way to make the sale happen if they can just buy some time. Such potential situations must be part of your employee training and orientation program. If, for example, a part cannot be expected to arrive in time to fix the equipment tomorrow, an employee should know not to mislead the customer by saying that it will. This seemingly simple fact appears to be a difficult concept in regard to customer service!

Steven Levitt and Stephen Dubner (2014) give us a good example of this struggle with honesty in their book *Think Like a Freak*. They suggest that the three hardest words in the English language are "I don't know." Consider the following example.

Imagine you are asked to listen to a simple story and then answer a few questions about it. Here's the story:

A little girl named Mary goes to the beach with her mother and brother. They drive there in a red car. At the beach they swim, eat some ice cream, play in the sand, and have sandwiches for lunch.

Now the questions:

1   What color was the car?
2   Did they have fish and chips for lunch?

3   Did they listen to music in the car?
4   Did they drink lemonade with lunch?

All right, how'd you do? Let's compare your answers to those of a group of British schoolchildren, aged five to nine, who were given this quiz by academic researchers. Nearly all the children got the first two questions right ("red" and "no"). But the children did much worse with question 3 and 4. Why? Those questions were unanswerable—there simply wasn't enough information given in the story. And yet a whopping 76 percent of the children answered these questions either yes or no (pp. 19-20).

Why would the children answer questions 3 and 4? Quite surprisingly, most of us can probably cite situations where we have experienced such deceptive responses. Perhaps we have even done it ourselves. We seem to think we should always have an answer, but sometimes we just have to admit that we do not know. Customers will respect that, *if* we continue with, "but I will find out."

Have you seen the 2002 movie *Catch Me if You Can?* The outlandish adventure is based on the true story of Frank Abagnale. Abagnale successfully performed cons worth millions of dollars before his 19th birthday. However, his scheming eventually led to his arrest and prosecution. It wouldn't have made for such entertainment, but telling the truth works better in real life!

Customers may believe you if you make up answers and state them with confidence, but eventually that will catch up with you and you will have lost your customers' trust, likely spelling the end of your job – or even your business. It is much more difficult to gain that trust back than it is to lose it. It is much more effective to be honest. If you don't know the answer, tell the customer that you don't know. But then follow the admission with an assurance that you will find out the answer. However, then you must have follow through and actually find out and report the answer to the customer, or, once again, you will lose their trust and respect.

Look at Me When I Talk to You

As we indicated earlier, if we are not looking at the customer, it may appear that we are not paying attention to what they are saying. In the United States it can be a simple sign of respect to look at someone when they are talking to you or you are talking to them.

Terry was at the Walt Disney World Resort visiting Korean exchange students who were working there as part of Disney's

International College Program. One student, who was working as a lifeguard, related the story of being yelled at, and reported by, a guest who had asked him a question while he was on duty. The guest was behind him, and he answered without looking back at her, making her angry for the disrespect she thought he was displaying. However, unknown to her, he was following his training, which required him not to take his eyes off the water at his station. (Perhaps stating that fact in answering the guest's question could have prevented the episode, but trying to think and multitask in a second language is quite a challenge!)

Have you ever been at a customer service desk trying to tell the organizational representative what your problem is but they were doing another task and would not even look at you? How did that make you feel? You probably felt disrespected.

As we just stated, sometimes a customer needs help in a store. Perhaps she has a question about a product or needs to find something. Imagine her seeing a group of employees talking together at the end of the aisle, but she cannot get their attention. Or, she may walk down to them and ask a question, but none of them responds or even looks at her. Customers are frustrated and feel disrespected when ignored in this manner. The employees could be in a personal conversation that should not be happening during work hours, but they could also be conferring about a work issue and just need a minute to finish the discussion. In that case, all it would take is a simple acknowledgment of the customer, perhaps stating, "One of us will be with you in just a minute." (Of course then they need to actually follow up and get to the customer within a minute or two.)

When Ed has a student come to his office for advising or to talk about a class project or issue, or even just to chat, he will put down what he is doing and look at the student. He also doesn't answer the phone while they are there. This is to give them the attention they deserve and to show them respect. Sometimes, when Ed is expecting an important call or has been dealing with an emergency, he needs to take a call right away. In these circumstances, he will tell the student that he might have to take a call. If it does happen, he excuses himself from the conversation, but then resumes full attention to them when the phone call is over.

Following this rule of demonstrating to your customers that you respect them and their time should be a simple matter. If you have carefully selected employees and have a staff with the "customer first" approach of the marketing concept, then hopefully your customers feel it. If you review complaints and suggestions and more than a few refer to circumstances like those we've covered, a little review in a meeting or during regular training sessions would be worthwhile.

Apply Rule #4: Show Respect

Give your customer undivided attention. Be honest. Admit your mistakes.

1   What procedures or training do you use to ensure that employees are truthful in their interactions with customers? Is "I don't know" encouraged? Gather six or seven employees from different areas and ask for anecdotes about such interactions and discuss how and why they occurred.

2   Do you know what your customers think about whether, or how much, you respect them? Is your position stated somewhere in publications, signage, or somewhere else the customer can see? If not, how can you succinctly state it, and where can you put that statement?

3   Make a list of simple things you can do to demonstrate respect for your customers. For example, some organizations greet customers as they come in the door. What specific things would make *your* customers feel respected throughout your interaction with them? You can find out more ways by asking them.

References

Levitt, S., and Dubner, S. (2014). *Think like a freak.* New York: William Morrow an imprint of HarperCollins Publishers.

Small, G., and Vorgan, G. (2008). *iBrain: Surviving the technological alteration of the modern mind.* New York, New York: Harper.

5

BE COURTEOUS AND KIND

"Treat everyone with politeness, even those who are rude
to you, not because they are nice, but because you are."
– Unknown

Be courteous and kind. It's such a simple, easy thing to do isn't it? So why does it seem so difficult? Why do we have to mention it? In January 2016, Rabbi David Wolpe wrote an article entitled "Why Americans Are So Angry About Everything." His article resonates with our discussion here about customer service. Wolpe says, "Much of our frustration arises in an age of unlimited expectation when atrocities and injustice are constantly paraded before our eyes." He goes on to say that, "Particularly galling is our understanding of unfairness" (Wolpe, 2016). Underlying much of what we have been saying about customer service is the idea of fairness. Customers want to know and feel that they are being treated fairly.

Perceiving unfairness makes people angry. Wolpe (2016) says, "Angry people are poor communicators and even worse listeners." It is difficult to understand each other's points of view when you are angry because you are not communicating your thoughts well and you are not listening

well. We have already discussed the importance of listening and the impact it has on customer service. Courtesy and kindness can go a long way in reducing the intensity of anger.

Shifting the Climate

The admonition to be courteous and kind is a common theme in kindergarten and elementary school classes. Learning goes much more smoothly if we are courteous and kind in the classroom, the hallways, the cafeteria, and on the playground. Sometimes it seems that we have lost a bit of this in our society in general. What ever happened to simple niceties like "yes ma'am" and "yes sir?" And unkindness spreads so quickly now with technology and social media. If customers are upset, they can (and often do) post scathing critiques on Facebook, Yelp, Twitter, or other social media. Dissatisfaction spreads quickly, and it takes a lot more good press to try to counter the bad.

If someone is rude to you, and you return the rudeness, it is just going to continue to escalate. For example, a hotel in Indiana received a bad Yelp review and charged the complaining customer's credit card $350. This, of course, did not improve the relationship with the customer nor encourage others to become future customers. Many small business owners have gotten even more aggressive, suing customers over negative reviews. The trend has been building so much that at least 25 states have passed laws preventing such anti-negative social media review practices (Covington, 2017).

If we are able to be nice in difficult situations, we may be able to shift the climate in the interaction toward a positive outcome. Also, if all of your employees are regularly courteous and kind when interacting with customers, fewer difficult situations will arise. Let's return to the Girl Scouts for a minute. You remember the scout motto is "Be prepared." In the 1947 Girl Scout Handbook, the motto is explained this way, "A Girl Scout is ready to help out wherever she is needed. Willingness to serve is not enough; you must know how to do the job well, even in an emergency" (Girl Scouts, n.d.). This means to look for opportunities to help. What a great customer service idea! And it is usually not that difficult to find ways to be helpful.

The Walt Disney Company, an acknowledged world leader in customer service, encourages cast members (Disney's term for all its employees) in every position to look for simple ways to "make a magical moment" for guests. Disney used what it called "The Four Keys" for many years to guide cast members, and recently expanded them to five. The Keys are Safety, Courtesy, Show, Efficiency, and Inclusion.

In cast member actions to make guests' experiences as enjoyable as possible, the second most important Key (after safety) is Courtesy. Guests are to be treated with kindness and respect. Cast members know they are encouraged and supported to do whatever they can to meet or exceed guest expectations.

Consider this example of the courtesy key at work for Disney. The Disney College Program is a semester-long internship program, with optional extensions making the experience potentially several months longer. College students complete the same training as permanent cast members. Terry's daughter completed the program during her undergraduate studies. She related to us a story that captures the way the Disney Keys are used to look for ways to please guests:

> *Some merchandise is only available in one or two places around the parks and resorts. We had a family in my store one evening and their son had wanted a particular plush character when they had shopped there earlier in the week. Unfortunately, we were out of stock that day, as it was very popular at the time. However, I had worked a shift in another shop that shared operations with our store, and I knew that both carried some of the same items. I told my supervisor and he called the other store. Fortunately, they did have the plush character in stock, so he arranged for the item to be transferred from their stock, then went and picked it up. The family was so ecstatic that they stopped by our store later just to thank us! The mother wanted to give us a hug! It was gratifying to see how important it was to them, although this item was not expensive at all.*

Lands' End, the clothing and home goods retailer, is just as renowned for customer service as Disney. Lands' End allows its customer service associates the freedom to make customers happy *however they see fit*. Among the values the company tries to instill in its employees is (Lands' End, n.d.):

> "A passion for the work you do. *Care for the people you're doing it for*. And a willing hand whenever there's need." (Emphases added.)

The retailer cites its founder in the values section of its website, stating his belief that "as long as you put your customers, employees, and community first, success would surely follow." The investment Lands' End makes in its people rivals Disney and is a great benchmark for anyone wanting to make strides in improving service. Service employees (Lands' End refers to them as "customer care specialists") for the retailer receive *over 65 hours* of training! (Lands' End, n.d.).

Nonverbal Elements, Smile, Greet People

Nonverbal communication can help you deliver on this rule as well. And one simple nonverbal act can make a big difference – smile. A simple smile can make a big difference in how a customer feels about the interaction. A smile can demonstrate you are happy to be working, pleased to be responding to the customer. Of course, a smile in response to an angry statement by a customer could be interpreted negatively, as if you are mocking them or do not care. In this case, it is the calmness and politeness that makes a difference – showing the customer that you are willing to try to address their situation through your words, demeanor, and welcoming body language. (See our website simplecustomerservicerules.com for ideas about smiling when wearing a mask as we have had to do during the COVID-19 pandemic.)

Smiling would be an easy way to alleviate some of the frustration we've mentioned previously for customers who are standing in line. Imagine their reaction if workers were courteous, looking at the customer, smiling and saying, "I will be with you in a minute." This small act can make a big difference in a customer's attitude and help the upcoming interaction go more smoothly. Making a customer wait for several minutes without even acknowledging them is disconfirming and can make a customer angry. Ed and his wife decided to try a fast-food restaurant that Ed hadn't tried since college. They went in a particular store and stood in line behind several other patrons who had already been waiting. Ed and his wife waited ten minutes and were never even acknowledged! They left the store. Do you think they are likely to try again?

Even on the telephone a smile can make a difference. Have you ever been interviewed via a phone call? Interview experts, such as interview consultants and bloggers Jeff Gillis and Mike Simpson, include among phone interview tips the advice of smiling during the call (Simpson, n.d.). We agree and believe the same advice holds true for customer service

over the phone. After all, in a way you are constantly "interviewing" to keep your job as a product and service provider to the customer on the other end of the line!

Ed recently bought a flagpole bracket from *The Flag Guys* and made a call to customer service during the process. He could *hear* the smile in the voice of the person who answered the phone. She was very nice, helpful, and pleasant to talk to. Ed wanted to send the bracket to his parents' address. This was no problem with this special request, and she even took the service a step further, asking if the receipt and information could go to that address or if it needed to be sent to him. In other words, she was anticipating his needs of not wanting his parents to see the receipt or receive the literature. Even though in this case it didn't matter, Ed was impressed that she thought to ask to make sure the experience was as pleasant and accurate for him as it could be. He actually enjoyed the few minutes on the phone with this representative and realized that he had a smile on his face as he hung up the phone. On the company's website (www.flagguys.com) you can read these words: "A live person answers!" and "Where They Still Say 'Yes Sir,' Yes, Ma'am' And Thank You For Your Business." This is simple kindness and courtesy!

Word Choice Makes a Difference

Choose words carefully. "Yes ma'am" and "yes sir" are certainly aspects of language demonstrating kindness and courtesy, but there is much more to appropriate language than this. For example, it is important to choose words that are meaningful to your particular audience. In some cases language needs to be more formal while in others such formality might be absurd. Whatever level of formality is right for the task at hand, service personnel should be polite and respectful. They should also be understandable.

Have you ever had computer trouble and called a technology specialist – either for the piece of equipment you own or at your workplace? Most of us have. How did they respond to you? Did they use language you understood, or did they use technical language that went beyond your ability to understand. Were they polite in their approach, or did they speak down to you like you were an idiot because you didn't understand? Imagine being told by your doctor she is prescribing a medicine for your rhinorrhea. Would you know what she was talking about? (That is the term for a runny nose.) Or what if a doctor told you your grandmother was suffering from atheromatosis. Would you recognize that diagnosis? Atheromatosis is a thickening of the arteries. Or maybe your doctor says you have arthralgia or glomerulonephritis or . . . . You get the idea. Appropriate language is language that is meaningful to the customer.

Once, early in his career, Ed taught an Interpersonal Communication class in a prison. At the time he was also a youth director at his church. Although many of the same concepts in the Interpersonal textbook were topics of discussion in his youth group, he had to talk about them a little differently to male prison inmates than he did to middle school students. This is true of nonverbal elements as well. Let's say you are selling insurance to a farmer and to a banker. If you go to the farmer dressed in a suit and tie, he may think you don't understand his business and what his issues are. You might better connect with more casual attire. However, if you meet the banker with that same casual attire, she may think you are not professional. She expected the suit and tie. Offering excellent customer service means that you understand the context.

Be Nice

Be nice. The Girl Scout motto at the beginning of this chapter to "be able to help out wherever needed" can remind us to look for opportunities to help customers. Remember Terry's story from Chick-fil-A in the introduction? The manager saw the confused look on Terry's face and immediately came to his table to find out if there was a problem. Then he took care of the problem quickly. A simple action, but it made a difference in Terry's family dining experience.

For a retail worker this could simply mean asking customers if they need help finding something in the store or offering product information to help them make a satisfying decision. Several times Ed has experienced an employee at his local auto parts store make a suggestion to bundle items in a particular way, or buy a different package for one item and put it with another, to save money. This was a simple thing to do, but it made Ed a happier customer. And, what the salesperson didn't know is that Ed is working on restoring a 1966 Mustang, so he will likely need more parts. This simple suggestion will likely encourage Ed to return to that particular store.

Apply Rule #5: Be Courteous and Kind

Acknowledge the customer. Smile. Use appropriate language. Look for ways to be nice.

1   How do your employees conduct themselves during interaction with customers? With fellow workers? Consider staging a role play during a training session to study how well they are communicating. Have two employees take turns being the customer and the service person. Have others serve as observers and take notes while watching the interaction. Afterward, have everyone compare notes and offer ideas for improvement. Allow some of those who were observing to then take turns as the customer and service person.

2   Do you know your customers' perception of how your employees act when in contact with them? If not, what are some ways you can find out? Perhaps contact a few customers who have taken the time to make comments and follow up with questions to understand areas for making positive changes. This will help your business and that customer will feel they are being heard, leading to positive feelings they may share with other potential customers.

3   What do you tell new employees about courteousness and kindness? How about your more experienced employees? Have they maintained a positive approach to being courteous and kind? Do they share insights with their less experienced counterparts? Make a list of what can you do to encourage such interaction and knowledge and skill sharing.

References

Covington, O. (December 21, 2017). Hill urging consumers penalized for negative reviews to contact AG's office. *TheIndianaLawyer.com.* https://www. theindianalawyer.com/articles/45689-hill-urging-consumers-penalized-for-negative-reviews-to-contact-ags-office. Accessed 11/16/20.

The Flag Guys. http://www.flagguys.com. Accessed 11/16/20.

Girl Scouts. https://www.girlscouts.org/en/about-girl-scouts/traditions.html#:~: text=Motto%3A%20The%20Girl%20Scout%20motto,The%20same%20 holds%20true%20today.

Lands' End. *About.* https://www.landsend.com/aboutus/values/. Accessed 11/16/20.

Simpson, M. (n.d.) Top 5 Skype interview tips (and the mistakes to avoid). TheInterviewGuys.com. https://theinterviewguys.com/skype-interview-tips/. Accessed 11/16/20.

Wolpe, R. D. (January 5, 2016). Why Americans are so angry about everything. *Time.Com.* https://time.com/4166326/why-americans-are-so-angry-about-everything/.Accessed 11/16/20.

6

FOLLOW DIRECTIONS

"It is absolutely necessary... for me to have persons that can think for me, as well as execute orders." – George Washington

Perhaps you remember taking a test in elementary school where the first direction was "read the entire test before answering any questions." Then when you read through the test the last item stated something like, "Now that you have finished reading everything, answer questions 1 and 2 only" (which were the aforementioned "read the entire test before answering any questions" and "put your name on your paper.") and continued with something like "Look busy so that others can continue to work without disturbance. Do not give a clue that you have completed the test." You would watch the other students (hopefully it wasn't you) feverishly working. Then you would gradually begin to hear students respond to instructions in the middle of the test like "loudly call out your first name when you get to this point" and stand up on your chair and shout "I am nearly finished; I have followed directions."

The point is, of course, that we should follow directions. In this case, that was to read the entire test first. This test was to emphasize one of the rules that had been part of our educational experience since preschool (like don't run in the hallway) – simply to follow directions.

You would think it would be easy to follow directions, and sometimes it is. Usually there is a reason for doing so. It was unsafe to run in the hall because we could hurt someone (or ourselves) if we ran into someone. It would seem apparent, too, that running with scissors is unsafe. Thus, following directions can be important for safety issues. Sometimes there are federal regulations that must be followed. For example, there are Federal Aviation Administration regulations that set requirements that must be met on commercial flights (minimum number of flight crew; briefing before takeoff concerning smoking, seatbelts, oxygen, use of electronics, etc.) that must be done (see faa.gov). Following directions can often actually be helpful to consumers. We are glad to have someone check our ID when we are using a credit card, for example. And we are glad when people stop at red lights!

Enhancing Customer Service by Following Directions

There are many good reasons to have policies, directions, guidelines, or whatever you may call a standardized approach your company has put into place for the services (and/or products) you provide. Safety is probably the top such reason that following directions can enhance customer service. Disney is known for top-notch service. In fact, through their Disney Institute they have trained many organizations how to adopt the Disney way to create everyday practices to satisfy customers, whatever the setting. In Disney's service standards, safety is the first item, the top priority. Without it, other potential benefits from a particular service can be rendered meaningless from injuries to customers or employees. Whatever you may be able to do for a customer must only be attempted after the situation is deemed safe for all involved.

Think about visiting one of Disney's theme parks. If you are on a roller coaster, you want to know that the employees have followed directions to make the ride safe, from the designers to the ride inspectors to the cast members operating it. If your family is having dinner in a park restaurant, you want to be assured that everyone has followed directions to make sure the food is cooked properly and is safe to eat. (This might especially be true for vendors through the park who are out in the hot sun.)

Sometimes regulations are an issue. Some services are quite complex, and service employees must work within the bounds of regulatory and/or legal frameworks to do the job. The airline industry is one that is heavily regulated. Think of other industries you interact with regularly. There are regulations for cell phone service, food service, educational institutions, and so forth. Your service improvement must take such situational features at all levels for your type of business into consideration when designing new processes or entire new services.

Problematic Policy Application – Following Directions to the Bitter End

But following directions as an excuse can be problematic. Saying, "it is policy" as a way to *avoid* addressing the problem will not satisfy the customer, and this is not how you will want to be remembered – as an organization that follows (or hides behind) policy no matter what.

Consider United Airlines (UAL) and two events in April 2017. The video that went viral of a passenger being forcibly dragged off a UAL flight by law enforcement is an example of adhering to "policy" no matter what. United needed four passengers to volunteer to leave the flight. United offered a cash incentive, hotel, and rebooking. However, no one

volunteered. So, United "randomly" chose four "volunteers." Three of the four peacefully exited the plane. The fourth, however, refused to give up his seat. He was a 69-year-old doctor and said he needed to see patients the next day. And though he had originally agreed, when he discovered he could not catch another flight out the same night, he changed his mind. After the incident, United issued a statement that began: "Flight 3411 from Chicago to Louisville was overbooked . . . After our team looked for volunteers, one customer refused to leave the aircraft voluntarily and law enforcement was asked to come to the gate . . . (Calfas, 2017)."

The video of this event shows the passenger screaming while being dragged down the aisle on his back by his arms. His glasses are askew, and his face is bloody. Other passengers are visibly upset and verbally expressing their displeasure. There are many things that are troubling here regarding customer service. First, usually airlines ask for volunteers at the gate *before* passengers are actually seated on the plane. Once you are in your seat, you don't expect to have to give it up.

The "general" policy is to randomly select volunteers if enough passengers don't come forward on their own. Two terms here are troubling. First, there is a priority system process airline use to remove "less important" passengers first (airline employees not being transported to another airport for work, then people who paid less for their ticket, etc.). If there are guidelines for whom to choose, then it isn't really random. The more troubling word here, though, is "volunteers." How can someone be a "volunteer" if they don't want or choose to do it? (If you or someone you know has been in the military you may have heard them refer to this as "voluntold.") Two days later, the saga continued, it was learned that the flight wasn't actually overbooked:

> United spokesman Jonathan Guerin said Tuesday that all 70 seats on United Express Flight 3411 were filled, but the plane was not overbooked as the airline previously reported. Instead, United and regional affiliate Republic Airlines, which operated the flight, selected four passengers to be removed to accommodate crew members needed in Louisville the next day. The passengers were selected based on a combination of criteria spelled out in United's contract of carriage, including frequent-flier status, fare type, check-in time and connecting flight implications, among others, according to United.
>
> (Bacon and Mutzabaugh, 2017)

UAL CEO Oscar Munoz sent a letter to employees "lauding the behavior of the flight crew in dealing with a 'disruptive and belligerent' passenger" (Bacon and Mutzabaugh, 2017). So, now a passenger who doesn't want to give up a seat he paid for is disruptive and belligerent?

Here was an early response by Munoz to the public:

> 'This is an upsetting event to all of us here at United. I apologize for having to reaccommodate these customers. Our team is moving with a sense of urgency to work with the authorities and conduct our own detailed review of what happened. We are also reaching out to this passenger to talk directly to him and further address and resolve this situation.'
>
> (Rosenthal, 2017)

"Reaccommodate?" Is that what you would call it if it happened to you – especially if you were forcibly removed from your seat and dragged down the aisle of the plane? We doubt it! The response to this incident cost United's CEO the opportunity of a planned expansion of duties to the airlines' parent company's board chairman. Ironically, Munoz had received an award from *PR Week* the previous month, naming him the communicator of the year.

UAL's reputation suffered for months after this incident, with multiple parodies of UAL on TV comedy shows and social media. *PR Week's* Editor in Chief commented that United's response would eventually be quoted as an example of how not to respond in a crisis. News stories featured other passengers who had been bumped; cases which would previously have been deemed inappropriate for such news segments. When you adhere to policy in strict ways that are not thoughtful or that do not incorporate common sense, you can aggravate (and we are being nice here) and disrespect customers. And strict adherence to policy without careful consideration or attention to specific situations can snowball and make matters worse from a customer service perspective.

The very next day after the customer (and PR) fiasco we just mentioned, United threatened to handcuff a passenger if they had to in order to get him to leave the plane. The passenger was told that the flight was overfull and they needed the seat for someone more important who had showed up at the last minute. Remember, like the doctor on the Louisville flight, this passenger was already seated. In fact, he had to get home early, so he had booked a full-fare first-class seat – about $1,000. He was already in his seat. He was a frequent flyer, but the other passenger had apparently flown more miles.

The airline "compromised" and put the passenger in economy class in a middle seat between a married couple in the middle of a nasty fight who refused to sit next to each other. They argued the whole flight – nearly six hours. This is what the passenger got for a thousand-dollar first-class ticket. United had switched planes because of a mechanical issue, and the smaller plane had fewer first class seats. That is understandable. But as we noted above, why not deal with that at the gate? Why wait until a passenger is already seated to bump them?

The passenger asked for a refund. A "corporate customer care specialist" apologized if his flight was unpleasant, but said there would be no refund, though he was offered a refund of the difference between the first-class and economy fare prices. The representative also said that despite a negative experience, UAL hoped for continued support because his business was especially important to them. The passenger said three different members of the crew apologized for how he was treated, but they told him they were unable to do anything (Lazarus, 2017). United, like many organizations, was so firmly locked into their positions that there was no room for empathy or common sense!

These are extreme examples, of course, but if you take a moment, we think you will see that *both* situations began as *simple customer service scenarios*. They escalated because of a chain of UAL personnel following policy instead of looking for simpler alternatives. Looking back at the loss of reputation and the many other costs, it would have been significantly cheaper to have sent the four passengers or the Louisville crew to their destination by first class on another airline! This could also have been the simple solution in the second incident as well. What situations in your business can you think of where, though you followed policy, it ended up being negative experiences? Can you think of simple solutions you could have developed at the time that would have not necessarily been strict adherence to policy but that would have preserved a positive image, saved your company money while also satisfying the customer?

There are certainly safety issues that must be followed if passengers are to arrive at their destination. Assigning the proper number of crewmembers is a safety issue. Ensuring the airplane is mechanically sound is a safety issue, and avoiding extreme weather along the route is a safety issue. Accommodating crewmembers for another flight, however, is not a safety issue. It may be policy to accommodate crew members, and might even be important for the airline, but from a customer service perspective, such a policy needs to be a little more flexible.

The United employees were just following policy. According to policy, they didn't do anything wrong. The results, though, were a PR disaster. Employees need to be empowered to deal with specific issues as they arise – not simply follow what is written in corporate policies. It is important to follow safety and governmental regulations, but a certain amount of flexibility should be built into policies to allow for empathy and common sense.

The bottom line is, how do you want your customers to view you and your organization? They want to feel safe, but they also want to feel cared for. There must be some flexibility, within reason, to be able to meet customer needs in a variety of situations, while still adhering to industry regulations. Common sense should be a part of the service design.

Creativity

Well-trained service personnel will have the knowledge and skill to come up with appropriate service offerings that may combine parts of

standard services instead of trying to fit a standard service provision in when it isn't appropriate. Just as good kindergarten teachers encourage exploring and seeing what a student can think of doing, *the best* service providers will match the service to the needs of a particular customer and setting.

Ensuring employees can indeed be creative in the application of services begins with your definition of the basic service(s) they will be expected to provide. From writing clear job descriptions to asking questions during the hiring process, you must enable *all* of your employees to be prepared to take the knowhow learned from orientation and training and apply it to individual cases of service needs. This aspect of being prepared is akin to the "empowerment" concepts popular in the 1980s and 1990s. That is, the service providers working for you should go to work each day knowing how to do the basics with confidence that their company and its leaders will back them up as they decide exactly what to do during individual interactions and service delivery. Their preparation, knowledge, and confidence will be apparent to customers. Remember the marketing concept from the first chapter? Being market-oriented is a good start!

Flexibility

Flexibility, bending the rules when necessary, goes hand in hand with creativity. Following company policy within reason can be a good practice. Following it everywhere and every time can be just the opposite. Besides understanding the services they'll be responsible for delivering, and the freedom to be creative in doing so, employees will also need to be able to decide when certain policies can be loosened if circumstances dictate.

> *Terry was returning from a business trip through London's Heathrow Airport when weather conditions delayed his incoming flight and he missed his connection. This turned out to be a good thing, because he experienced the excellent customer service provided by British Airways' (BA) Flight Connections. Instead of standing in a line and eventually talking with an agent about rebooking options, clear signage guided passengers to the Flight Connections area near international arrivals. A uniformed agent came to him and looked up his flight itinerary on her tablet. She then took his boarding passes and passport and asked Terry to wait right where she had met him. After 8 or 10 minutes, she returned with his new itinerary, boarding passes, and a voucher for a meal during the two-hour window until his new flight began boarding. British Airways was as*

flexible as possible, with no flight change charges and Terry's needs anticipated and met.

As flexible and professional as British Airways was for Terry's travel disruption, his experience with an automobile company and its dealership, which we will not name here, was on the other end of the spectrum!

Terry and his wife bought a new SUV from the company's local dealership, and they liked everything about the vehicle. Within two years, however, two major problems convinced them it was the last time they would buy that brand! First, the purchase included a complete vehicle service every 5,000 miles. This included tire rotation and inspection, oil change, and topping off any necessary fluids. After only 30,000 miles the service manager told them there was a problem with the tires—all four needed to be replaced!

It turned out that the camber was off, causing all tires to wear excessively on the inside edge (The camber is the angle of the tires to the road). The dealership itself had been inspecting and rotating the tires for a year and a half, with no comments about the excessive wear that had been well underway. The cost for the camber repair and a new set of tires was over $700 – for a vehicle still under warranty!

A second problem that promised to be even more expensive soon appeared. This one was related to a design flaw in one part of the emissions system. The result was that a pipe related to that system would become clogged with road debris and trigger the computer to signal engine maintenance was needed. Though the vehicle continued to run, the signal caused its cruise control not to work, which was very inconvenient for long drives.

The same service manager showed Terry the manufacturer service bulletin that had been issued in October of the year he had bought the car. The vehicle was only four months old when the bulletin was issued. The service bulletin stated that the problem would be covered under warranty. However, Terry's car did not experience the flaw's related problems until after the warranty had expired because of mileage. At first, neither the dealership nor the manufacturer showed any flexibility in addressing this problem for which the solution was a $1,100 part and $500 of labor. After much complaining, Terry was offered $500 from the manufacturer's regional service manager. Instead of opting for the repair, Terry found a local auto repair shop that could clean and reset the problem when it occurred.

The response of the dealer and the corporate office of the manufacturer in Terry's experience ensured that he would have no further consideration of the company for any future vehicle purchases. How simple it would have been to bend the rules slightly to cover the issue shortly after the warranty had actually expired. It would likely have been much more cost effective for the company as well. Terry could have been a satisfied customer who would return to purchase his next vehicle (he went to another automaker for his next purchase). His family and friends have heard the story, and many have chosen to consider other brands as well.

Common sense

The care in hiring, training, and equipping of your service personnel should include encouraging them to challenge policy when such policy is detrimental to customer needs, again, within reason. The customer may not always be "right," but you should consider the customer valuable. Even if the customer is not 100% correct, is there validity in their

concern? Put yourself in their place. What would you want and think was reasonable in such a situation? Try to understand how they feel and seek creative solutions that work within your organizational goals but also leave the customer satisfied.

Herb Kelleher, the co-founder of Southwest Airlines, suggested that you should hire for attitude, and then train for skill (we wondered if perhaps he had coached Frank Martin at some point!). If you go to the Southwest Airlines website (southwest.com) and scroll down and click on "About Southwest" and then click on "why fly Southwest," you can read the following words:

> **Customer appreciation day is every day.** Our Customers mean everything to us. We like to think of ourselves as a Customer Service company that happens to fly airplanes. From booking your trip to the moment you deplane, it's our mission to make your travel experience a great one.

Southwest gives their employees some latitude when dealing with customer service issues. A quote from Gary Kelly, the current Southwest CEO, can also be found on the website: "Our people are our single greatest strength and most enduring long term competitive advantage." Remember the Post Office example in Chapter 2? Treating your employees right and giving them a certain amount of flexibility is an important step toward achieving excellent customer service.

Apply Rule #6: Follow Directions

1   Are safety guidelines, regulations, etc., prevalent in your industry? If so, how do you ensure that your employees are up to date on them? List your top three safety practices. How do your efforts at promoting safety impact your overall customer service?

2   How much freedom do your employees have in solving problems that might not fit neatly within your set of guidelines? In a training session, set aside time to discuss what employees understand their flexibility to be within the organizational policies. Make sure they understand your guidelines in terms of what you expect of them in terms of flexibility in customer service problem-solving.

3   Are your customers aware of your treatment of safety issues? If you have won awards for your operations from compliance agencies, trade associations, and the like, are they prominently displayed so your customers are reassured? Check your physical location, web sites, social media sites, and so forth to be sure you are prominently displaying these recognitions, and that they are consistent across platforms, and that they are up to date.

References

Bacon, J., and Mutzabaugh, B. United Airlines says controversial flight was not overbooked; CEO apologizes again. https://www.usatoday.com/story/news/nation/2017/04/11/united-ceo-employees-followed-procedures-flier-belligerent/100317166/. Accessed 11/16/20.

Calfas, J. (April 10, 2017). Video shows man forcibly removed from overbooked united flight. *Time.com.* https://time.com/4732783/united-airlines-man-doctor-removed-overbooked-flight/ Accessed 11/16/20.

Lazarus, D. (April 11, 2017). Column: United passenger threatened with handcuffs to make room for 'higher-priority' traveler. https://www.latimes.com/business/lazarus/la-fi-lazarus-united-low-priority-passenger-20170412-story.html. Accessed 11/16/20.

Rosenthal, D. (April 11, 2017). What was United's CEO thinking? *Chicago Tribune.com.* https://www.chicagotribune.com/opinion/letters/ct-united-ceo-apology-oscar-munoz-20170411-story.html. Accessed 11/16/20.

Southwest.com.

7

ALWAYS DO YOUR BEST

"I do the very best I know how – the very best I can; and I mean to keep on doing so until the end." – Abraham Lincoln

Do you remember the 1980s Ford commercials that claimed, "Quality is Job 1?" Quality is vital for successful organizations and satisfying customer relationships. As children we were told always to do our best. Ed

remembers when one of his daughters was concerned because one of her grades wasn't quite up to her usual standard. She was afraid he would be mad at her. His question to her was, "did you do your best?" Sometimes our best isn't what we would want it to be, but it is our best at that time.

Customers understand that – if we truly are doing our best. Improvement over time is a part of quality control. In business we are faced with new competitors using new approaches, from new services and service system improvements to new technologies and current technology applied in novel ways. We have to adapt to such changes in the competitive landscape and do our best – over and over again. Hopefully our best becomes better and better over time.

Quality and Continual Improvement

A simple adage is to check with your customers to see how you're doing. In academia, students evaluate instructors at the end of each semester, and supervisors use those evaluations to conduct faculty performance reviews. It is not unusual to have very glowing evaluations along with evaluations from students who were obviously very unhappy – within the same class! This can occur for a variety of reasons: anticipated grade, personality clashes, subject matter, and whether the class is required or an elective, just to name a few. What is important in interpreting these evaluations is consistency. If most students identified a particular area that needs improvement, then the instructor and his/her supervisor can take a closer look and determine what can be done to improve performance. If most students indicated they were satisfied with a particular aspect of the class, the instructor should make sure any appropriate element(s) of that aspect is incorporated into the next class. Also, he or she should explore ways to improve it and make it even better. For outliers, it is important to try to determine *why* a student had such an extreme opinion (either positive or negative) compared to the average. Adjustments can be made to address any underlying issue(s) that caused such a strong response.

This approach is a good one to use for a business as well. Have you ever filled out a comment card at a restaurant or an online survey from a retailer and then nothing seemed to happen? If a business makes an effort to collect customer comments and seriously evaluate them, then it needs to make customers aware that their opinion is being valued. Carefully reading such comments, looking for things customers recognize you are doing well and complaints about areas where you are coming up short, can lead you to the adjustments necessary to return to meeting or exceeding customer expectations. Contact customers during this process to let them know you have read and/or heard their input and valued it. When they know that you have listened, it is far more likely they will solidify the relationship with you; they will know you are trying to improve to serve them better.

Gaps Model

Whatever the feedback from customers, organizations should also seek to improve over time based on environmental factors. New competitors may appear with new approaches to satisfying needs and wants. Current competitors may introduce other service innovations, new technology will become available, and new social media applications will be launched. All of these require businesses to evaluate what they are doing and contemplate how they can improve. In short, companies need to *benchmark* – i.e., compare their own processes and performance metrics to industry standards, and to standout service providers' best practices. Typical dimensions examined include quality, time, cost, and, of course, customer satisfaction.

Research to see what other organizations are doing better than they did before. Be aware and involved in activity in trade associations and conferences. Being well-informed and up-to-date on competitors, industry trends, etc., can help you keep doing your best at higher and higher levels of excellence.

How exactly can you do all of this? You may feel that every piece of advice above is great, but that the resulting information will be difficult to work with, coming from so many areas of your business and competitive environment. Fortunately, there is a model that can be very useful for organizing the information that will help you in your continuous improvement of service delivery – the Gaps model. At the end of the chapter, we provide a template you can use to apply the Gaps model in your own organization by considering how the seven rules can help you focus within the Gaps model's elements, leading to ever-higher service quality levels.

Gaps Model of Service Quality*

Regarding service quality . . .

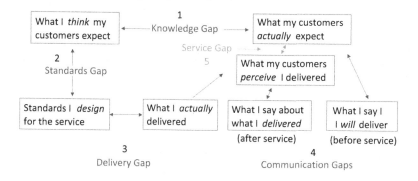

Figure 7.1

* Adapted from Parasuraman, Zeithaml, and Berry (1985), "A Conceptual Model of Service Quality and Its Implications for Future Research," *Journal of Marketing*, 49 (4), 49–50.

The Gaps model for service improvement is a tool you can use to focus on those key areas where great service is achieved – the same areas where service can fall short of customer (and your!) expectations. Let's take a brief look at this model, first presented by Parasuraman, Zeithaml, and Berry (1985).

The overall aim of service of any kind is to provide the promised action(s) at the level expected by the recipient. Of course, as we noted earlier, exceeding customer expectations can propel an organization into an elite cadre of excellent service providers, such as the status Disney or Nordstrom occupies. The most important "gap" featured in the model is shown as Gap 5 in the model here. Gap 5 is known as the *service gap*, which simply means that the customer perceives the service you delivered is below the level they had expected. The aim of the model itself is to help service managers narrow any such difference, either by improving service quality so that the gap is narrowed (rarely can we expect to completely eliminate any particular gap) or by making sure we communicate clearly so that customer expectations are realistic given our current capabilities.

Interestingly, improvement efforts are not aimed directly at the service gap itself. That's because it is not very prescriptive to state, "We must improve our service to better meet or exceed expectations." Rather, the Gaps model has four "sub-gaps" *for which specific data can be collected and specific actions can be taken*. The goal is to narrow each of these sub-gaps. Individually and collectively such improvements will then narrow the service gap. The sub-gaps are as follows: (1) the knowledge gap, (2) the standards gap, (3) the delivery gap, and (4) the communication gap. Let's look closer at each of these and how they interrelate.

Knowledge Gap

The knowledge gap represents the degree of understanding the service provider has about the expectations customers have for the service being studied. Areas of misunderstanding, missing information, or outdated data are three possible sources of difference between what you think customers want and what they actually want. Narrowing the knowledge gap requires constant attention on several fronts. Your customers' tastes may change slowly over time, for example, without you becoming aware of it.

Only when complaints increase or sales fall off do you notice when, of course, it can be more difficult to repair the damage. The best service providers stay in constant contact with customers, getting feedback, asking simple questions about satisfaction, and going further, say with in-depth interviews with a sample of customers. Currently, you may have six or seven social media accounts, all with good traffic, but if you don't interact with your customers regularly to detect, acknowledge, and head off potential service failures, and understand customer expectations, they may as well be ten-year-old e-mails stored in a filing cabinet! Besides communicating with and studying your own customers, you also need to stay at the forefront on trends for your particular industry and type of business. This means being an active member of appropriate trade associations, chambers of commerce, Rotary clubs, and the like. It also means studying your competitors to monitor what types of service innovations and challenges they are introducing and facing.

The various elements you determine to be important regarding your particular customers and competitors should include you entering that data into a Fishbein model (or other model) and updating it regularly. Note trends, whether positive or negative, and think about how you could counter the negative and capitalize on the positive. Follow up with customers; ask them how you can improve to better meet their wants and needs. As you implement such improvements and then collect data after they've been in effect you should see customer responses that are more positive than before.

Standards Gap

You can set better standards for the service you'll deliver by focusing on just a few important areas. Study customer expectations and try to determine how they might be changing. Interact with your peers in other organizations to find out what problems they are facing; these might start to appear in your own operations. Seek out any other information that can help by attending local business meetings, such as Rotary, Chamber of Commerce, and trade and professional associations. These actions will help you be confident about the procedures and policies you design for your service operations. From the training you create for your service personnel to the service descriptions your customers will see in your stores to content on your websites, you'll base decisions on solid information about the value those seeking your services are expecting.

Unfortunately, even if one has perfect knowledge, it doesn't mean that such knowledge will be successfully translated into service standards. This is Gap 2, the Standards Gap. Inexperience, lack of training, lack of talent, even lack of time, all can leave the statement of what will be provided short of the ideal. Making sure decision-makers have up-to-date training, staying current with general expectations in your industry, and monitoring your competitors (especially your strongest ones) can help assure you are turning the knowledge you have accumulated into solid standards that both your employees and customers can count on. Earlier in this chapter we described benchmarking. Consider using that technique here as well – a detailed study of standards set by companies known for their excellent service, even ones not in your own industry. An interesting aspect of this practice is that such companies often don't mind sharing with others who are not their direct competitors. The Walt Disney Company even sells such information – via its Disney Institute seminars on customer service.

Delivery Gap

For many of us this gap (#3) is the most familiar, and the most personal. In fact, when we think of particularly good or poor service, *the point of delivery is where we often focus*. Although customer criticism or praise is focused here, and can thus provide a starting point for improvement or redesign, remember the other gaps. Like those other gaps, delivery is just one area where improvement can be made. In delivering a service of any type, there is a point at which the service delivery person, an automated system, or some combination of the two and the customer are in direct contact. Whether you are signing up for an online college course or stepping up to a fast food counter, you will use the process designed with the intention to provide the appropriate service at the right time and place. Unfortunately, even if you are using a well-programmed touchscreen at a McDonald's restaurant, or you are directly interacting with a Disney cast member, everything doesn't always go perfectly well. Humans are imperfect and, whether the touchscreen needs cleaning or the order is mixed up with another customer's meal, service companies need to be ready to overcome deficiencies. The technical term in services research is "service recovery." If done well it can solidify a customer relationship.

For those instances where the delivery gap exists on a more regular basis (for example, let's say a high proportion of the complaints and/or suggestions from your customers entail the service person seeming to be in a hurry) the service provider must track down the actual source of the problem and fix it. Some common areas where service delivery is below the intended and expected standard are poor training, long hours, too few service personnel available, and miscommunication.

Remember the four Is concept described in Chapter 1? For the *Inventory* you have to balance the number of service providers (people and/or automated systems) with the expected number of customers in a given period. This is much like planning for any type of workload for any type of business, from manufacturing to pure service delivery. Training your employees to deliver the quality service you have designed and communicated to your customers is a necessity to avoid one type of delivery gap. Companies consistently ranked high on customer service by definition have a delivery gap narrower than average. Thorough training, such as Lands' End provides its service reps, is highly important. As the retailer states on its website, "We built our company on the belief that every customer deserves our absolute best."

Communication Gap

The things we write and say to our customers before, during, and after service is provided can be as important as the service delivery itself. This is especially true as the type of service tends to be more complex, meaning customers *need* more explanation, in terms they can understand, about what exactly was done for them.

The communication gap (Gap 4) can occur in several forms. For example, when we do not communicate well regarding the service standards we designed we can set up false expectations among our customers. This can in turn lead to reactions of "so what" if we have set standards too low or to customer disappointment when we regularly miss the mark because we have overstated our service abilities.

Another way the communication gap appears is when a service is completed but the customer does not clearly see the results, or even misunderstands what we just did for him/her. When a haircut is completed, a salon customer can look in the mirror and see whether the intended look has been achieved. When you take your car in for repair and get it back, depending on the type of problem you were having, you may not be able to determine if it is running better, despite having just spent $500! This is why good auto repair service providers explain what will be done and why *before* the job is started, and then go over what was done and why afterward. Accompanying this bookend approach is a detailed listing of the parts used and the service hours needed, leading to the final total cost. The best repair shops explain their work in non-technical terms. Though your service may not seem like rocket science to you (even if it actually is!), you cannot assume your customers will understand every detail and technical term on their own. Be prepared to explain, in writing or in person, what, how, and why particular service steps or work were done.

Summary

The Gaps model is not some magical device that can permanently fix service problems for your organization. However, if you have a desire to fulfill customer wants and needs, and seek to understand ways you are falling short in doing so, then this model is a tool that can focus your efforts on improvements in areas that matter to your customers so you can always do your best. Even the best can face service shortfalls and can gain value from applying the model to detect and examine gaps. For example, consider Terry's service failure and recovery experiences with Disney.

My family was at Disneyland, in line for Toy Story Midway Mania, a popular ride-through arcade attraction. After waiting for about 40 minutes, with 25 minutes to go, a cast member came out to announce that the ride was down and that it would not reopen any time soon. Further, he began handing out special fast passes (FastPass is a Disney innovation that allows its guests to choose a window of time when they can come back to an attraction and have little or no wait) and telling guests that these were good for any ride in the park. Unfortunately, an (apparently) arbitrary wait time was chosen—at a certain point one guest received a pass and the next person in line did not. Although that seemed to go a bit against the Disney way, what happened next made it pale in comparison! We chose to use our passes for one of the park's most popular attractions, Radiator Springs Racers, where two cars travel at high speeds around a track themed after the popular Pixar Studios Cars movies. This is one of our favorite attractions, but we usually only ride it once because wait times are so long and fast passes are all gone early in the day. Two young cast members working the Cars attraction looked at the special passes and then at each other. "We can't take that. I don't recognize that type of pass," one of them said, handing the passes back to us. No amount of explaining or asking them to call to find out persuaded them. In fact, at one point they exchanged a glance with each other that seemed to imply we had made up the entire story! This remains one of the biggest disappointments my family has experienced with Disney parks anywhere in the world.

Contrast that negative service experience with one Terry's family had on the other side of the country the following year.

We were fortunate to be in the Magic Kingdom park during the soft opening of the Be Our Guest restaurant's new breakfast hours. Besides eating in the dining rooms themed after the Beast's castle from the Disney animated classic film, we were excited about the added bonus of being able to enter the park prior to its regular hours, as breakfast hours started at 8:00 a.m., an hour before the park opened. It was fascinating to walk through the empty Main Street and over into the equally quiet Fantasyland where the restaurant is located. Having experienced excellent meals at this restaurant on two prior visits for lunch we wanted to see how the new breakfast option compared. After ordering, we were seated and awaited our meals. In the meantime a server came by with a tray of complimentary pastries that were delicious. Our expectations were growing for a fantastic breakfast! Our daughter's friend was with us this time and it was her first time in the restaurant. Thus we were *enjoying the surroundings and watching her experience it for the first time, while we waited for our food to come. After a while, we noticed a group seated next to us had finished their breakfast. They had arrived about the same time as we did, so we asked our server about the delay and she said she would check. A different server came by a few minutes later and we asked if she too could check. The answer came back that they didn't know what was happening; however, they brought another tray of pastries for us while we waited. We did not enjoy these as much. Finally, our food came out, just as a second group from the same neighboring table as before were finishing their meal—nearly an hour had passed since we had ordered! Shortly after the food arrived so did some "Disney magic"—in the form a dining room manager. He profusely apologized for the long delay, explaining that they had been experiencing some process breakdowns as they worked out the kinks in the new breakfast service. He comped our meals (this being a Disney theme park the bill would have been over $80!) and then gave us a handwritten form that served as a fast pass for any attraction, similar to what we had received at Disneyland the previous year. This time, however, we had no issue with using the passes. With Disney's premium prices, losing an hour in the park is no small matter for guests. The ability of being able to, in essence, give back that time in the form of a fast pass enables them to recover from service failures in a customer-pleasing way. (That is, assuming it ensures that all cast members are knowledgeable about these special-issue passes!)*

What mechanisms in *your* service delivery system can be utilized for service recovery? Do all of your employees know what to look for if a customer comes in after receiving some type of service certificate or coupon from a different employee, perhaps at another site? Are service failures recorded so an analysis can be done, whether with a system you use now or with the Gaps model? Communication is key – not only with customers, but among coworkers as well.

Apply Rule #7: Always Do Your Best

Check with customers to see how you are doing. Work on continuously improving over time. Communicate. Communicate. Communicate

1   What incentives do you have for employees to perform at a high level? Do your competitors have such incentives as well? How do yours differ from theirs? Make a list of how you will find out.

2   If you have an employee incentive system do you know if your employees are actually incentivized? What are their thoughts about the system? Have you asked them? Get your employees together or create an email group, etc., and ask them what they think.

3   The Gaps model can be applied via the seven rules we have offered here. The mechanisms you had in place before reading this book can be strengthened with the concepts and models we have discussed in this book. If you have a system for gathering information from employees, customers, and third parties you can use a template like the one below to continuously monitor and correct any weak areas. The template is available on the website as well.

If you do not have a system, spend some time thinking about how you can gather input from customers and employees. Common areas for such data include comment cards in physical facilities, e-mails, webforms, and recorded service calls. Mine these for ideas. A simple start can be to categorize and add up the terms customers use. Work first on the most frequent ones. Follow up by contacting a few customers and asking for their help in improving your service. Look for places where you need more information or where knowledge you have needs more detail before you can take action. Let's say, for example, that out of 100 comments 20 mentions are made of employees not following directions, that they seemed to be "winging it" during the service provided. Focus on those cells where you can improve based on this particular aspect of the customer experience. Let's say you choose two such cells – Be Prepared and Delivery and Follow Directions and Standards. You could then have a meeting with all service personnel (or all employees for smaller

Table 7.1 The Gaps Model applied via the Seven Rules

	Knowledge	*Standards*	*Delivery*	*Communication*
Come to class prepared				
Complete assignments neatly and on time				
Pay attention				
Show respect				
Be courteous and kind				
Follow directions				
Always do your best				

organizations) and discuss those areas of the matrix regarding the issue. Go over knowledge and standards and get input from employees on how to improve in those focused areas.

Reference

Parasuraman, A., Zeithaml, V., and Berry, L. (Autumn, 1985). A conceptual model of service quality and its implications for future research. *Journal of Marketing*, 49(4), pp. 41–50.

APPENDIX

Communication Exercise

Ten common terms will be discussed – five terms of probability and five terms of time. We have run this exercise many times over almost two decades, and always (and by always we mean 100% of the time) there has been a significant range on at least some of the terms that contributes to a lively discussion concerning our use of these common terms.

Miscommunication Exercise Common Terms Used

Answer for these words in terms of probability (i.e., between 0% and 100%).
Always _____
Never _____
Probably _____
Usually _____
Often _____
Answer for these words in terms of time (i.e., number of minutes, hours, days, etc.).
ASAP _____
Soon _____
Today _____
Tomorrow _____
Right away _____

Conducting the Exercise

Begin with the probability terms. Each term is read aloud and displayed in the classroom. Participants are prompted to record each term and then their own interpretation of the probability it represents. For example, the trainer might say, "Please write each term and then a probability representing what it means to you. For the first term, write 'always' on your paper and then a number beside it that represents what percentage of the time it means to you. If you say you 'always' do something, a certain way, or you use the word 'always' in speaking to someone, what probability does it mean to you between 0% and 100%?" Following this introduction and clarifying example, the other four terms are presented.

Once the probability terms are completed, the trainer announces, "OK, now let's move on to some other terms. This time, you'll be recording the amount of time each word or phrase means. The amount of time can be measured in whatever unit you believe is appropriate, from seconds to hours to days and weeks." Then the first term is written on the classroom display, again with a clarifying example. The trainer might say, "The first term is 'ASAP' which of course means 'as soon as possible.' So please record 'ASAP' on your paper and then an amount of time that it means to you. If someone tells you to do something 'ASAP,' what length of time do you think they mean? Remember to include the amount of time, including what unit you're using, for instance, 10 seconds, or 6 hours, or 2 weeks, or 3 months, etc. for this and the other terms I'll be showing you."

And so the trainer again proceeds to present the terms one at a time, with participants recording their interpretation of the length of time each term represents. After all ten terms are displayed, participants are prompted to ensure they have numbers recorded and not just a definition (e.g., for "probably" someone might have recorded "may or may not" where an actual probability is the proper response, such as 50% or 75%).

Once all participants have recorded the ten terms and their interpretations, the trainer announces that it is time to look at the results and moves to where he or she can record the responses on the display device (PC keyboard if projector is used, standing by a whiteboard or flipchart, etc.). For the first term ("always"), the presenter can ask the class if anyone has "100%" as a response. Usually (but not *always*!) there will be one or more such responses and the trainer records "100 to the right of the term, leaving room between it and the term for a second (lower) number. The trainer should next ask the class if anyone has *less than* 100%. This is the point when some participants begin to realize that there is something unexpected going on. Although there are occasions when no response is received to this inquiry (i.e., meaning that *everyone* has recorded "100%" for the term "always"), it is quite common to have responses of some lower number.

The trainer should not comment on any such differences yet. Instead, he or she moves on to each remaining term, asking for and recording the highest and lowest probability, and then longest and shortest length of time for the second set of terms. The trainer might choose to personalize and add some fun to this process. For example, the trainer might ask a particular student for his or her response, then ask the class if anyone has a higher number (this would be the opposite for responses with expected lower number responses, such as "never" or "ASAP"). Alternatively, the trainer can ask if someone has a particular number and then prompt the participants for lower or higher responses ("Does anyone have 25%?" or "Does anyone have an hour or less?" or "Does anyone have more than two days?"). This method can create a fun, auction-like atmosphere.

After recording the low and high responses for all ten terms, the trainer can then focus on some of the larger ranges for a particular term(s). The leader or participants may describe possible scenarios of miscommunication in customer service based on such differences in interpretation. One example might be an employee at a retail establishment who tells a customer that the manager will be with them "right away." The trainer can posit that the employee has a "within the hour" understanding of "right away" while the customer thinks this means the manager will be with him or her in less than five minutes. An hour waiting to talk to a manager can seem like a very long time to a customer. Many participants have their own favorite examples of these terms (or similar ones) and problems that have ensued from using them. (For example, once, when conducting the exercise during an MBA class, one of our participants reported that his firm had banned the use of the term "ASAP" within the company!)

The trainer concludes the exercise with a debriefing. Listing lessons the experience teaches is a good way to emphasize the effectiveness of the exercise in improving communication by avoiding miscommunication. The trainer can state some of these examples and/or solicit lessons to take away from the participants. At a minimum, the following main points should be made clear in closing the exercise session: (1) use actual numbers to say what you mean, (2) ask questions to clarify when you hear the terms from this exercise (or similar terms) being used, (3) know that the terms are used *purposefully* at times (such as when the user is unsure about something and wants to buy some time).

We have conducted the communication exercise many times and have encountered a wide range of responses even in very small groups (as few as five participants).

Active Listening Exercise

In an effort to understand how it feels to be listened to (or not listened to) try the following exercise; it is adapted from http://criteriaforsuccess.com/active-listening-exercise/.

The trainer should assign partners for this exercise or have the participants choose their own partner. One will be the speaker and one will be the listener. You will do two rounds using the same partners.

In the first round, the speaker is to share a customer concern with the partner (who could be a sales person, customer service agent, manager, etc.). The job of the "listener" in this case is to do everything possible to ignore the speaker (customer). Allow 90 seconds for this. End the activity at 90 seconds, and reflect on it. Ask participants – both speakers and listeners – how they felt during this exercise. Discuss the various feelings shared.

In round two, repeat the scenario with the same people in the same roles. Only this time, the listener is to listen as if the speaker's concern is the most fascinating thing they have ever heard. End the activity again after 90 seconds, and reflect on it. Ask again how participants – both speakers and listeners – felt this time. Make sure to address the differences in feelings between the two rounds.

We are certain that you will discover that listening well not only means that the information is exchanged and understood, but that both parties – speaker and listener – feel better about the interaction.

Resources

Government-Provided Resources

Centers for Disease Control and Prevention (CDC), small business resources and information, https://www.cdc.gov/coronavirus/2019-ncov/community/guidance-small-business.html

Benefits dot gov, official benefits website of the U.S. government, https://www.benefits.gov/help/faq/Coronavirus-resources

U. S. Small Business Administration, small business resources and information, https://www.sba.gov/page/coronavirus-covid-19-small-business-guidance-loan-resources

Business-Provided Resources

Google, g.co/smallbusiness, "Here to help small business." free tools and resources to get online, connect with customers, and more

Facebook, tips, training, and other resources to help small businesses stay open and connected to customers, https://www.facebook.com/business/resource

American Airlines, the company's protocols and news, http://news.aa.com/coronavirus/

Chick-fil-A, the company's "Safe Service" guiding principles, https://www.chick-fil-a.com/corona-virus

Disney, the company's protocols and news, https://disneyworld.disney.go.com/experience-updates/

Nu Look Home Design, home design and remodeling, innovating remote consultations and contactless services, https://nulookhomedesign.com/

Trade Association and Industry Resources

Chain Store Age, a leading provider of retail news and analysis, https://chainstoreage.com/

Nation's Restaurant News, a leading resource for business intelligence in the foodservice industry, https://www.nrn.com/

Restaurants Rise, information and insights to help those in food service navigate the new normal https://restaurantsrise.com/

Salesforce dot com, leading customer relationship management (CRM) platform https://www.salesforce.com/

Food Management, trends and best practices, products and solutions that connect deeply with the noncommercial foodservice professional https://www.food-management.com/

Supermarket News, competitive intelligence, news, and information for retailers, manufacturers, brokers, analysts, association executives and others connected to the supermarket industry https://www.supermarketnews.com/

Additional resources are available at simplecustomerservicerules.com

CREDITS

Introduction

Photo I.1 Image courtesy of Chevron Heritage Center
Photo I.2 Photo by Terry Holmes
Figure I.1 Figure by Terry Holmes

Chapter 1

Figure 1.1 Figure by Terry Holmes
Photo 1.1 Photo by Wonderlane on Unsplash.com
Photo 1.2 Photo by Claudio Schwarz | @purzlbaum on Unsplash.com
Table 1.1 Table by Terry Holmes

Chapter 2

Photo 2.1 Photo by Robin L. Martin-Holmes
Photo 2.2 Photo by Nick Fewings on Unsplash.com
Photo 2.3 Photo by Alex Motoc on Unsplash.com

Chapter 3

Photo 3.1 Photo by Yalamber Limbu on Unsplash.com
Photo 3.2 Photo by Mimi Thian on Unsplash.com
Photo 3.3 Photo by LinkedIn Sales Navigator on Unsplash.com
Photo 3.4 Photo by Magnet Me on Unsplash.com

Chapter 4

Photo 4.1 Photo by Ed Brewer
Photo 4.2 Photo by Cytonn Photography on Unsplash.com
Photo 4.3 Photo by Austin Distel on Unsplash.com

Chapter 5

Photo 5.1 Photo by Ryan Snaadt on Unsplash.com
Photo 5.2 Photo by LumenSoft Technologies on Unsplash.com
Photo 5.3 Photo by Dayne Topkin on Unsplash.com

Chapter 6

Photo 6.1 Photo by Nick Morales on Unsplash.com
Photo 6.2 Photo by The Creative Exchange on Unsplash.com
Photo 6.3 Photo by Ekaterina Z. on Unsplash.com

Chapter 7

Photo 7.1 Photo by John Benitez on Unsplash.com
Figure 7.1 Figure by Terry Holmes
Table 7.1 Table by Terry Holmes

INDEX

Printed in the United States
by Baker & Taylor Publisher Services